Supporting Mathematical Thinking

Edited by Anne Watson,
Jenny Houssart and Caroline Roaf

 David Fulton Publishers

 **NASEN**

David Fulton Publishers Ltd
The Chiswick Centre, 414 Chiswick High Road, London W4 5TF

www.fultonpublishers.co.uk

First published in Great Britain by David Fulton Publishers in association with the
National Association for Special Educational Needs (NASEN)

NASEN is a registered charity no. 1007023.

David Fulton Publishers is a division of Granada Learning, part of ITV plc.

British Library Cataloguing in Publication Data
A catalogue record for this book is available from the British Library.

ISBN 1-84312-362-2

Copy-editing by Jenny Shelley, *Write to the Point*
Designed and typeset by Kenneth Burnley, Wirral, Cheshire
Printed and bound in Great Britain

Contents

Preface

The context of most of the work described in this book is UK schools during a time (the late 1990s) when Years 1 to 7 were supposed to be following the National Numeracy Strategy, with the requirement that all primary children should have a 'numeracy' lesson every day. This should usually have three parts: a mental and oral starter and a plenary discussion (but see Chapter 9 by Julie Anghileri for some further detail). In secondary schools the daily lesson is not imposed. Curriculum support materials have been issued to all schools containing schemes of work and lesson plans. Also connected with the Numeracy Strategy are materials offering guidance to support pupils with specific needs in mathematics lessons (DfES, 2001). The materials are aimed at teachers and teaching assistants and offer guidance for supporting pupils with five areas of need: dyslexia or dyscalculia; autistic spectrum disorders; speech and language difficulties; hearing impairments; and visual impairments. This strategy is being evaluated over the early years of its implementation. In the book we sometimes refer to it simply as the 'strategy', the 'framework' or as 'numeracy'. None of the content of the book is, however, specific to this context. All of it relates to a broader view of the mathematical learning of schoolchildren and is thus pertinent to other countries and other educational structures.

Education is rife with quasi-technical terms which are used confusingly as definitions, professional shorthand, policy definitions and everyday expressions by different groups of people. Some terms which are seen by some to be non-controversial can be value laden and discriminatory for others. We have picked a gentle path through these and made some editorial decisions as follows:

We have tried to avoid gendered words except where talking of someone who is clearly of a particular gender. Where gender is used more generally we have followed the fact that most teachers, particularly in primary schools, are female.

We expect the terms 'students', 'pupils', 'children' and 'learners' to make sense to all readers and have used them as appropriate, and probably interchangeably in many places. We have, however, tried not to call anyone a 'low attainer' as this does not seem to us to be an appropriate way to speak of a person, particularly in a book about how particular levels of attainment need not be seen as a fixed, predictable outcome of education. Instead we talk of 'low attaining students' which places attainment as a current state, which may change, rather than a characteristic. This is not ideal, but the more sensitive alternatives we could find were cumbersome. We do not mean to imply anything about 'potential'.

Another common educational term we have avoided is 'ability' since it is often used without any qualification . . . 'ability to do what?' we would ask. Chapter 3, by Ann Dowker, shows that the term 'low ability' – as used to describe a weakness in mathematics – masks very specific difficulties which might be identified and overcome with careful teaching.

The expression 'bottom set' is the professional shorthand for the classes containing the students who have most difficulty with mathematics. In some schools these are also called 'boosters' or 'springboards', names which derive from various substrategies of the strategy. While finding all of these expressions unpleasant, since they carry with them so many assumptions, expectations and beliefs, we have nevertheless retained the phrase 'bottom set' where it relates to how schools use the expression.

Now to more mundane matters which require terminology. In some chapters, we refer to paid adult helpers in school classrooms. There are a number of acronyms by which these can be known: LSAs (learning support assistants), TAs (teaching assistants), CSAs (classroom support assistants) and support staff. We have used the abbreviation LSA to refer to all paid adults in classrooms other than teachers. As we write, it has been suggested that they should be redescribed and retrained as TAs – but the writing of this book took place while the role was still seen as supporting learners, hence our decision to retain the term LSA.

Finally, several of these chapters were first published as articles in the journal *Support for Learning* and some have now been updated for this book. We thank, on our authors' behalf, all the schools, learners and teachers who have contributed to the work on which this book is based. All real names of people, and some schools, have been changed.

Special thanks go to our copy-editor, Jenny Shelley, for patient and generous help.

Anne Watson
Oxford University

Jenny Houssart
The Open University

Caroline Roaf
Oxford Brookes University

Reference

DfES (2001) *The National Numeracy Strategy. Guidance to support pupils with specific needs in the daily mathematics lesson.* London: DfES Publications.

Contributors

Mundher Adhami is a research worker at the Department of Education and Professional Studies of Kings College London. He studied geophysics at Moscow and Durham Universities and worked in computer dynamic modelling before switching to teaching mathematics in London schools. He then moved to curriculum development and formative assessment for the Graded Assessment in Mathematics (GAIM) project at Kings College London and the GCSE examination syllabus. Since 1993 he has been involved in research and development in the Cognitive Acceleration in Mathematics (CAME) series of projects for Key Stages 3, 2 and 1, and the associated teachers' professional development programmes. He co-authored *Thinking Maths* (Heinemann, 1998), and *Primary Thinking Maths* (BEAM, 2002) and contributed to *Learning Intelligence* (Open University Press, 2002).

Afzal Ahmed is Professor of Mathematics Education at University College Chichester and is Director of the Mathematics Centre. Afzal has extensive experience of teaching at secondary school level as well as in higher education. He was a member of the Cockcroft Committee and has directed numerous research and development projects concerned with improving teaching and learning and increasing mathematical capabilities of people of all ages. He has worked closely with the various government and non-government departments concerned with learning, teaching and assessing mathematics both in this country and internationally. He is an elected member of the International Commission for the Study and Improvement of Mathematics Teaching (CIEAEM) and has contributed actively to various organisations and associations concerned with teaching mathematics. He is a joint editor of *Teaching Mathematics and Its Applications*, a journal of the Institute of Mathematics and Its Applications.

Julia Anghileri lectures in the University of Cambridge Faculty of Education. She has written and contributed to numerous publications and has international recognition for her research on children's learning of multiplication and division. As a consultant she works for the National Numeracy Strategy (NNS) and Qualifications and Curriculum Authority (QCA) as well as a number of local education authorities.

Ruth Barrington works at the School of Education at Bath Spa University College, where she is a senior lecturer in Primary Mathematics Education. She is particularly interested in exploring approaches which encourage fruitful involvement for all children during whole class interactive teaching, particularly in plenary sessions.

Ann Dowker is University Research Lecturer at the Department of Experimental Psychology, Oxford University, and College Lecturer in Psychology at Keble College and

Wadham College. She carries out research in developmental psychology. Her primary interest is mathematical development, especially individual differences in arithmetic, and interventions for children with difficulties in arithmetic. She has devised, and is piloting, the Numeracy Recovery intervention scheme (currently funded by the Esmée Fairbairn Charitable Trust) in collaboration with seven Oxford primary schools. She is co-editor with Arthur Baroody of *The Development of Arithmetic Concepts and Skills* (Erlbaum, 2002).

Cathy Hamilton is a principal lecturer at Bath Spa University College where she has worked in primary mathematics education for about six years. She works within the primary mathematics team and also has responsibility for the PGCE Primary Programme. Before that she was a deputy head teacher and SENCO in a primary school. She is interested in mathematics-specific research but also in more generic issues to do with education and, in particular, Initial Teacher Training policy and practice.

Tony Harries is a lecturer in mathematics education at the School of Education at Durham University. He has taught in both primary and secondary schools in the UK and in Bangladesh. After teaching for eight years at Bath Spa University College he moved to Durham in 1999. His main interests at present focus on the use of computer environments to explore young children's facility to represent numbers and number operations. In addition he is involved in developing links between Durham University and educational institutions in Southern Africa.

Jenny Houssart has worked in primary schools, advisory work and in teacher education. She writes regularly for the *Times Educational Supplement* and is currently a research fellow at the Centre for Mathematics Education, Open University. Her main research at the moment is carried out in 'bottom' mathematics sets in primary schools. Other research interests include mathematical tasks and early algebra. She is the author of *Low Attainers in Primary Mathematics* (Routledge Falmer, 2004).

Rosalyn Hyde now works in teacher training and curriculum development following ten years in school as a secondary mathematics teacher. She works part time for the Mathematical Association as their Professional Development Officer and also at the University of Southampton where she is part of the secondary mathematics PGCE team. As part of her work for the Mathematical Association she coordinates T3 (Teachers Teaching with Technology) for England and Wales. This is a programme offering professional development and support for teachers in using graphics calculators and data-loggers to enhance the teaching and learning of mathematics. She is also a visiting research fellow at University College Chichester.

Mike Ollerton began teaching in 1971. Between 1986 and 1995 he was head of mathematics at a school in Telford and here, alongside colleagues, he was responsible for devising problem-solving based schemes of work to support teaching and learning in mixed-ability groups across the 11–16 age range. Since 1995 he has worked at St Martin's College, Lancaster, teaching mainly on PGCE and MA courses. He carries out a significant amount of in-service work, focusing in particular on issues of inclusion and teaching mathematics using accessible, problem-solving approaches without using textbooks or published schemes. He is author of *Learning Teaching Mathematics Without a Textbook* (Association of Teachers of Mathematics, 2002).

Pat Perks works as a lecturer in mathematics education at the University of Birmingham. Before joining the university she worked as a teacher, head of department and

advisory teacher in Birmingham. Her interests lie particularly with technology, calculators (especially with infants), spreadsheets and the interactive whiteboard, but she
enjoys all aspects of mathematics. She is co-author with Stephanie Prestage of *Adapting
and Extending Secondary Mathematics: New tasks for old* and *The National Numeracy
Strategy for Key Stage 3: A practical guide* (David Fulton, 2001).

Stephanie Prestage works in mathematics education at the University of Birmingham,
working with pre-service and in-service teachers. She spent a number of years as head
of faculty in a large London comprehensive school before moving to Birmingham.
She has a wide range of interests in mathematics teaching, mathematics education and
professional development, and has worked on a range of research projects. She is co-
author with Pat Perks of *Adapting and Extending Secondary Mathematics: New tasks for
old* and *The National Numeracy Strategy for Key Stage 3: A practical guide* (David Fulton,
2001).

Caroline Roaf spent 20 years as a special educational needs coordinator in three
Oxfordshire secondary schools. For most of that time she combined a career in schools
with research and writing. Her doctoral thesis examined factors leading to successful
inter-agency work for children and young people. She has held grants from the Joseph
Rowntree Foundation, the Calouste Gulbenkian Foundation and the Teacher Training
Agency. Since 1999 she has been a part-time senior lecturer at Westminster Institute of
Education, Oxford Brookes University. She is editor of *Support for Learning*, a journal
of the National Association for Special Educational Needs (NASEN). She is the author
of *Coordinating Services for Included Children: Joined up action* (Open University Press,
2002).

Anne Watson is a lecturer in mathematics education at the University of Oxford, where
she is involved in the development of secondary mathematics teaching. She taught in
secondary schools for 13 years, during which she was involved in curriculum development, devising activity-based teaching which enabled all students in comprehensive
schools to gain a GCSE in mathematics. Her research interests include the integration
of mathematical thinking into ordinary life. She has written extensively on mathematics teaching, and has worked with teachers and teacher educators in many other
countries. She is co-author of *Inclusive Mathematics 11–18* with Mike Ollerton (Continuum, 2001), and *Questions and Prompts for Mathematical Thinking* with John Mason
(Association of Teachers of Mathematics, 1998).

Honor Williams is a reader in mathematics education and the Director of Teacher
Education at University College Chichester. Honor has had considerable experience of
teaching at secondary school level and at higher education level. She was the Assistant
Director for the government-funded Raising Achievement in Mathematics Project
(RAMP) and has subsequently overseen a number of research and development
projects, particularly concerned with assessing and evaluating mathematics and
continuing professional development for teachers of mathematics. Her current work is
concerned with developing and communicating evaluative approaches to help teachers
raise their own standards. She also has extensive experience of writing pupil and
teacher material and has made a substantial contribution to writing and editing the
Mathematics Centre publications.

Introduction

CAROLINE ROAF

This collection of articles originated in a special issue of *Support for Learning* published in February 2001, entitled 'Supporting Mathematical Thinking' and guest edited by Anne Watson. The rationale for that issue, and subsequent issues focusing on other curriculum areas, has been based on the need to recognise the enormous amount of work going on in mainstream classrooms to promote inclusive approaches by subject specialists. This book celebrates their expertise. Many mainstream colleagues who would never ordinarily think of themselves as 'special educational needs educators' appear to be just that in their close observation of how children, in all their diversity, think and learn. It seems in these instances that inclusion has become a reality: an indication of the bridge building going on between 'special' and 'mainstream' as proposed in the 1997 Green Paper and its sequel, the 1998 *A Programme for Action* (DfEE, 1998). In these, the stated aim of the government is to:

> . . . promote the inclusion of children with SEN within mainstream schooling wherever possible. We shall remove barriers which get in the way of meeting the needs of all children and redefine the role of special schools to develop a network of specialist support.
>
> (DfEE, 1998, p. 5)

These aims could, with equal force, be applied to the relationship we have seen developing within mainstream schools in recent years between special educational needs teachers and mainstream colleagues. Teachers, passionate about their subjects and passionate about their students' capacity to learn, have developed new and creative ways of teaching and learning. We can thus seek inspiration, on the one hand, from Bruner's famous dictum:

> With respect to making accessible the deep structure of any given discipline, I think the rule holds that any subject can be taught to any child at any age in some form that is honest and powerful.
>
> (Bruner, 1972, p. 122)

and, on the other hand, by the current government's view that:

> Good provision for SEN . . . means a tough-minded determination to show that children with SEN are capable of excellence.
>
> (DfEE, 1997, Foreword)

These inclusive approaches appear too, to be based on the principles, also clearly articulated in the 1997 Green Paper, of equal opportunities and of high expectations of all children. Whether the writers of the chapters in this book think of themselves as 'inclusionists' is open to question, of course. But whether consciously or not they, as teachers, researchers and teacher educators, had been sufficiently stimulated *intellectually* by the effects of inclusive practice to want to find out more. For them, the challenge was just too interesting, and often just too much sheer fun, to ignore. For SENCOs, putting resources into these classrooms paid dividends in terms of fresh ideas and as examples of success on which the process and progress of inclusion depends. Classrooms in which proficiency approaches to mathematics are adopted are, for researchers, subject coordinators and heads of department, the seedbeds for research and for school and staff development.

A common factor in the chapters has been, therefore, the manner in which the teachers and researchers operated: focusing on the fully educational (in the original Latin sense of *educare* – to draw out) application of intellect to the problem of developing mathematical thinking among one's pupils. Each article in the original journal issue demonstrated reflective minds at work, relying on close observation, willingness to understand the student's thinking processes, and patient commitment to students over long periods of time. As every reader of the *Times Educational Supplement*'s series 'My Best Teacher' will be aware, an inspired, committed and observant teacher lives in the memory for a lifetime.

An additional, and no less important, reason for presenting a collection of articles by maths specialists under the NASEN imprint is to encourage a meeting of minds in terms of the further development of existing links, for example via conferences and the internet, between subject specialists and special educational needs teachers. In both fields, there is much to be gained from stronger cross-curricular links between teachers. As yet this is not easily achieved, with subject associations developing their own approaches to inclusion which may or may not reach, still less be designed in collaboration with, the increasingly diverse and sometimes geographically dispersed teachers of children with special educational needs. The appointment, in 2001, of a joint project officer between the National Association for Special Educational Needs (NASEN) and the Association for Science Education (ASE) was a welcome initiative (Fenton, 2002), as was the joint conference between the Association of Teachers of Mathematics (ATM) and NASEN, held in 2002.

Nonetheless, in spite of some improvements, notably the work undertaken for the QCA by subject specialists at pre-National Curriculum levels (the P levels), there is a perennial problem of fragmentation (see, for example, Lawson, Marvin and Pratt, 2001; QCA, 2001). Those working in special education cannot expect to develop expertise in every subject or indeed every individual form of 'learning difficulty'. They must therefore rely on developing a set of principles governing their action across a very wide range of activity. Some of these have been touched on already: equal opportunities and high expectations. The latter encourages teachers to look forward to what they and their students might achieve, rather than to past failures. Nor does having high expectations imply the setting of endless unachievable targets. Indeed the failure-inducing language of targets is not appropriate here, when what might be achieved is so necessarily and invitingly unpredictable.

A further principle current among many special educational needs teachers has been to focus first on success and what has been understood. Only then, having secured for the child a position of maximum confidence and strength, are they invited to think about what might be achieved next and how one might get there. Adults, who respect one another, do not on the whole initiate conversations with others with blunt comments about faults and shortcomings, and should not do so with children. The thrust of much recent legislation encourages approaches based on respect for human rights applying as strongly to children as to adults, and in the classroom as well as in society at large. The 1995 Disability Discrimination Act, now updated in the 2001 Special Educational Needs and Disability Act (SENDA) to bring education within its remit, is based on the principles of equality, dignity and respect. Likewise, Article 12 of the 1989 United Nations Convention on the Rights of the Child (UNCRC) (for a full version see UNICEF UK, 1995) asserts that children have the right to say what they think and be listened to by adults when adults make decisions that affect them. In the ways of working described in this book these basic values shine through.

Another challenge to much traditional thinking concerns the question of where the sources of 'learning difficulties' or 'barriers to learning' lie. In recent years special needs education has moved away from thinking based on 'deficit' models of disability towards the view that disability is socially constructed. Thus those disabled by steps into a theatre are no longer disabled if lifts are provided. The use of language promoted by the disability rights movement (for example, a person would now be described as a 'wheelchair user' rather than 'wheelchair bound') is gradually becoming familiar in common parlance. Furthermore, from 2004, legislation will place a duty on planners to remove or alter a physical feature, or provide a reasonable means of avoiding the physical feature. Neil Smith of the Centre for Accessible Environments expresses it in this way:

> When described in terms of the social model we shift the 'problem' from:
> - the private to the public arena
> - the subjective to the objective
> - an individual to collective responsibility
> - something which we can do little about to something we can feasibly resolve.
>
> (Smith, 2002)

Since so much of the work of special educational needs educators is taken up with the removal, adaptation or avoidance of metaphorical 'barriers', I make no apology for dwelling here for a moment on physical barriers. The Warnock Report (DES, 1978) famously declared that:

> The purpose of education for all children is the same; the goals are the same. But the help that individual children need in progressing towards them will be different. Whereas for some the road they have to travel toward the goals is smooth and easy, for others it is fraught with obstacles.
>
> (para. 1.4)

Twenty-five years ago it was the children who had the obstacles:

> Broadly our task has been to consider how teaching and learning can best be brought about where there are children who have particular obstacles to overcome, whether these are primarily physical, sensory, intellectual or emotional.
>
> (para. 1.5)

Today we can take a different perspective. To what extent, for example, is it the curriculum subjects that have their own unique special needs, rather than the children? Indeed it is an interesting question to pose among teachers, who have little difficulty identifying the special needs of their subject and find that exercise illuminating. A group of modern linguists with whom I discussed this agreed that, fundamentally, their subject's special needs centred on having the courage and confidence to speak. The ability to listen and memorise was also considered important. The special needs of science are likely to be in the areas of sequencing, logical reasoning, observation and sustained attention over a period of time. The highly abstract nature of mathematics and the focus on the recall of procedures learnt in elementary education give it very considerable special needs. As we have seen in the articles presented here, these 'barriers' form the core of the challenge to those seeking to support mathematical thinking. In this sense it is not surprising that we see teachers developing an interest in young people held up by a barrier to learning or, as we might now begin to express it, the special needs of the subject. It is from the students facing these 'barriers' to learning that teachers will learn most. This turning of tables is a relief all round: suddenly the student previously seen as a 'problem' provides the opportunity for the teacher to learn and succeed as well as the student.

The National Curriculum Handbook (DfEE/QCA, 1999) suggests as much. The inclusion statement outlines:

> . . . how teachers can modify, as necessary, the National Curriculum programmes of study to provide all pupils with relevant and appropriately challenging work at each key stage. It sets out three key principles that are essential to developing a more inclusive curriculum:
>
> A.   Setting suitable learning challenges.
> B.   Responding to pupils' diverse learning needs.
> C.   Overcoming potential barriers to learning and assessment for individuals and groups of pupils.
>
> (p. 32)

Thinking of this kind has been much advanced by Susan Hart, a well-known and influential researcher among special needs and mainstream teachers of whatever subject specialism. Her re-evaluation of the concept of 'differentiation' and 'support' has led her to propose, in *Beyond Special Needs* (Hart, 1996), that the SEN label be dropped once and for all. Instead, Hart asks us to consider and choose between three contrasting approaches 'when a child's learning triggers concern and a desire to intervene in some way to facilitate development . . .' (p. 110). Diagnostic thinking looks 'for something wrong that can be put right'. Differential thinking 'looks for ways to match provision more closely to the child's individual needs and personal learning styles' and emphasises assessment. Innovative thinking by contrast:

> . . . involves searching out new possibilities for responding to a situation – or child's learning – that is causing concern through probing analysis of our existing thinking and understandings. It involves going to work on our existing thinking in such a way as to generate new insight into what might be done, beyond what is currently being done or tried, to support and enhance the child's learning.
>
> (Hart, 1996, p. 111)

In her more recent work Hart outlines in some detail five questioning 'moves' as a framework for innovative thinking. These five moves (making connections; contradicting; taking a child's-eye view; noting the impact of feelings; postponing judgement in order to find out more) prompt teachers, she suggests:

> . . . to draw on the vast reservoir of relevant knowledge about the dynamics of learning and teaching which they have acquired through experience, training and reading and to use this knowledge creatively in seeking to gain new insight into some aspect of their practice that they have identified as requiring further thought.
>
> (Hart, 2000, p. 9)

Although there was no article in the original *Support for Learning* issue, and there is none here, which formally applies these five moves, most bear the marks of such a process. Taken as a whole, the writers exemplify Hart's determination to support teachers in their attempts to 'think through teaching'. As in the work described in this book, Hart's thinking has arisen from close observation, attention to every detail and nuance of a student's approach to learning, and a relationship with, and respect for, children which regards them with optimism, with interest and, in her words, 'postpones judgement'. How can this intensity of observation, this commitment to the young people and determination to ensure they understand and learn, be best achieved? Significantly, in several instances, the contributors to this book show their willingness to slip flexibly between the role of researcher, assistant and teacher as the vagaries of classroom life dictate. This flexibility seems an appropriate response to the complexity of what is needed here: knowledge of the subject, teaching skills, an understanding of each student as a learner, as well as the ability and time to observe, to reflect and to share insights with colleagues. As Jenny Houssart observes (Chapter 5), assistants often know individual children well enough to judge when, for example, 'encouragement to move forward is likely to be appropriate and when it is best avoided'. But this knowledge of the children needs to be complemented by knowledge of the subject. Getting this balance right would appear to underlie the emphasis in this book on the value of professional development and collaboration.

Two introductory chapters set the parameters for the rest of the book, focusing on the development of reflective practice particularly among groups of teacher working in collaboration, and on the close observation of the kind familiar from the work of Hart (1996; 2000). Afzal Ahmed leads with an illuminating discussion of some of the 'shifts in culture' which have taken place since the publication of the Low Attainers in Mathematics Project (LAMP) report in the mid-1980s (Ahmed, 1987) and, post-National Curriculum, the Raising Achievement in Mathematics Project (RAMP) of the early 1990s (Ahmed and Williams, 1992). Ahmed stresses the need for continued staff development, especially that which includes space for research and reflective practice in collaboration with others. Anne Watson echoes these themes in Chapter 2, in which she 'catches' lower attaining students in the act of thinking mathematically: they can and do, as she and other contributors to this book demonstrate.

References

AHMED, A. (Project Director) (1987) *Better Mathematics*. LAMP Report. London: HMSO.

AHMED, A. and WILLIAMS, H. (1992) *Raising Achievement in Mathematics Project*. RAMP Report. West Sussex: ChIHE/HMSO.

BRUNER, J. (1972) *The Relevance of Education*. Trowbridge: Redwood Press.

DfEE (1997) *Excellence for All Children: Meeting special educational needs* (Green Paper). London: The Stationery Office.

DfEE (1998) *Meeting Special Educational Needs: A programme of action*. Sudbury: DfEE.

DfEE/QCA (1999) *The National Curriculum: Handbook for secondary teachers in England*. London: HMSO.

FENTON, A. (2002) Editorial. *Support for Learning*, 17(4), 154–5.

HART, S. (1996) *Beyond Special Needs*. London: Paul Chapman Publishing.

HART, S. (2000) *Thinking Through Teaching*. London: David Fulton.

LAWSON, H., MARVIN, C. and PRATT, A. (2001) Planning, teaching and assessing the curriculum for pupils with learning difficulties: an introduction and overview. *Support for Learning*, 16(4), 162–7.

QCA (2001) *Planning, Teaching and Assessing the Curriculum for Pupils with Learning Difficulties: Science*. Sudbury: QCA.

SMITH, N. (2002) Paper presented on behalf of the Centre for Accessible Environments at the DDA and Access to Education Premises Conference. London, 17/7/02.

UNICEF UK (1995) *The Convention on the Rights of the Child*. London: UNICEF.

WARNOCK REPORT (1978) *Special Educational Needs, Report of the Committee of Enquiry into the Education of Handicapped Children and Young People*. London: HMSO.

CHAPTER 1

Is there a substitute for experience in learning?

AFZAL AHMED and HONOR WILLIAMS

It is a good thing to experience everything oneself, he thought. As a child I learned that pleasures of the world and riches were not good. I have known it for a long time, but I have only just experienced it. Now I know it not only with my intellect, but with my eyes, with my heart, with my stomach. It is a good thing that I know this.

(Hesse, 1973, p. 78)

It is now more than 15 years since the publication of *Better Mathematics* (Ahmed, 1987), the report of the Low Attainers in Mathematics Project (LAMP, 1983–6). At an early stage of LAMP, it became clear to all involved that low attainment was not only a problem for pupils in the 'bottom 40%' attainment range. Changes in teaching approaches were encouraging *all* pupils to become more involved in their mathematics and to surpass traditional expectations at every level. The problem became one of under-achievement across the age and ability range.

It is interesting to note that, as indicated in the original report, it is still not difficult to find classrooms where children:

- lack confidence in the subject
- spend the majority of their time reproducing their teachers' examples with different numbers
- answer only other people's questions
- ask, 'What am I supposed to be doing then?'
- fail to connect their mathematics with other subjects or with their life outside school, even when they are successful in their mathematics lessons
- dislike mathematics, seeing it as irrelevant and boring
- spend most of their time mystified.

(Ahmed, 1987, p. 3)

Some may believe that, as considerable resources have been spent on national initiatives to improve the teaching of mathematics since the report, the situation outlined above may now only be observed infrequently. In this chapter we will attempt to re-examine the essence of ideas and approaches underpinning LAMP and *Better Mathematics*. We will focus on what we considered was at the heart of improving the mathematical experience and confidence of pupils, that is, 'Teachers must be actively involved in the process of professional development in order to develop their confidence, motivation, autonomy and professionalism both in providing for pupils' needs and in terms of their own mathematics' (p. 38). Adrienne, a teacher of pupils with moderate learning difficulties, gained confidence in enabling her pupils to find their own solutions to mathematical problems, choose their own methods of working and become independent learners. She found that her pupils had confounded many stereotypes about children with moderate learning difficulties.

> In the past two years my own views of mathematics, how people learn it, and how it should be taught have changed. The stimulus for these changes has been a combination of my own experiences of doing mathematics and the discovery that my pupils could do mathematics in ways that I had not appreciated before. As I have altered the way I teach mathematics, I have found pupils have been more highly motivated and have demonstrated skills that I had not suspected they possessed.
>
> (Bennett and Williams, 1992, p. 63)

Perhaps one of the most significant shifts in climate from 15 years ago is that the main challenge for us then was to articulate the notion of teaching being a research activity and to embed relevant theory into practice. We feel now that a greater hurdle will be to unpack the rhetoric associated with effective teaching and learning of mathematics as well as continuing to develop and support confident and competent practitioners. Some of the characteristics for achieving this have been documented by the external evaluator of the Raising Achievement in Mathematics Project (RAMP):

> In supporting teachers in their professional development RAMP has enabled them to take responsibility for:
>
> * research
> * curriculum development
> * enhancement of pupils' learning.
>
> It has enabled teachers to realise that they are the prime agents of change and that the shape of classroom practice in the future can be revolutionised by them. As such the following statements from *Better Mathematics* are endorsed.
>
> *Statement 16*
> Where research is embedded in teachers' own experiences it holds more meaning and credibility for them.
>
> *Statement 18*
> No imported curriculum development exercise can be effective without working commitment and teacher involvement.
>
> *Statement 12*
> Teacher enthusiasm for and personal engagement in the processes of mathematics will greatly enhance the mathematical experience of their pupils.
>
> (Ahmed and Williams, 1992, p. 18)

The importance of professional development has assumed greater emphasis more recently since the National Numeracy Strategy (DfEE, 1998) has provided all schools with an abundance of materials to support the teaching of mathematics. In addition, in *Qualifying to Teach: Professional Standards for Qualified Teacher Status and Requirements for Initial Teacher Training* (DfES, 2002), the focus on continuing professional development is clearly articulated:

> They are able to improve their own teaching, by evaluating it, learning from the effective practice of others and from evidence. They are motivated and able to take increasing responsibility for their own professional development.
>
> (para. 1.7, 6)

LAMP and RAMP managed to enable teachers to minimise the conflict between the practical demands of classrooms and to take a wider educational perspective on teaching and learning, particularly of mathematics. However, with the escalation in both teacher and pupil materials, many teachers find themselves in a parallel situation to that of many pupils – 'I can't do all of this, Miss – just tell me if I need to add or multiply'; similarly for teachers – 'There is too much to choose from, just tell me what activity / text will work best with my pupils.' This led us to revisit the following description of teachers' professional development from the RAMP Report, 'How teachers have become more discerning with regard to in-service provision, published material and other resources' (Ahmed and Williams, 1992).

> It seems, therefore, that there is a need to revitalise within the current context how teachers are able to develop themselves, as individuals or in groups, so that both pupils and teachers can:
> * become confident in their own mathematical resources and in their power to understand, use and generate mathematical ideas
> * extend their own knowledge by developing their own skills of self-teaching and enquiry, and
> * learn to value their own and others' expertise.

Moore and Morrison (1998) have argued consistently in their book that:

> The personal development of teachers is the most important factor in developing provision to meet special educational needs. This personal development will not take place unless teachers, as individuals, participate in the development activities of their colleagues. The inability of some teachers to 'share' experiences in this way is, we believe, the biggest stumbling block to progress.
>
> (p. 63)

Reflections on the prevailing educational thinking and 'political' context during LAMP and RAMP

Both LAMP and RAMP involved teachers in:

* working together, discussing, sharing and reflecting on classroom experiences, both successful and unsuccessful

- working in groups, focusing on specific issues, including the examination of a number of previous relevant curriculum development and research projects, both in mathematics and in other curriculum areas
- developing strategies for in-service work in their schools and with other teachers
- exploring mathematical situations and evaluating possible outcomes
- evaluating the effectiveness of commercial resources in the classroom
- exploring the creative use of calculators and microcomputers
- working with other teachers on in-service courses
- working with other teachers in their classrooms.

LAMP was one of the post-Cockcroft projects charged specifically to exemplify, through practice, some of the major recommendations and principles outlined in the Cockcroft Report (1982). The Cockcroft Committee was set up in 1979 in response to the 'Great Debate' on standards in education following the then Prime Minister James Callaghan's Ruskin College speech in October 1976. Following this speech the curriculum and the assessment system as well as teachers' performance came under increasing public scrutiny and criticism. Teachers' freedom to decide, within a broad framework, what to teach, when to teach a particular topic and how to teach it, was being challenged. McCulloch and McCaig (2002) exemplify this freedom by quoting Bonham Carter in 1947.

> Teachers are free to frame their own curriculum and to choose their own text-books within a wide general framework. This freedom inevitably develops in them a sense of responsibility and an initiative which could not exist if they were robots, subject to a rigid, centralised control.
>
> (p. 249)

The Cockcroft Report, instead of recommending a curb to this freedom, re-emphasised teacher responsibility, the widening of teaching approaches and the importance of continuing professional development opportunities for teachers to be able to exercise the above, both professionally and effectively.

In the spirit of the Cockcroft Report and the HMI publication, *Mathematics from 5 to 16* (DES, 1985), the project's philosophy was deeply rooted in the thinking of pragmatists such as Charles Sanders Peirce (1839–1914) and John Dewey (1859–1952). According to Magee (1998), Peirce's central contention was that knowledge is an activity and that we acquire knowledge by participating and not by being spectators:

> We are moved to enquire, to want to know, by some need or lack or doubt. This leads us to evaluate our problem-situation, to try to see what it is in the situation that is wrong, or missing, and ways in which that might be put right. This scheme applies even when our problem is a purely theoretical one.
>
> (Magee, 1998, p. 186)

Dewey considered all acquisition of knowledge as a human activity. Confronting a difficulty of some kind leads us to formulate a problem. This is often far from straightforward, but it is vital and may require several stages before clarity is achieved, and is followed by seeking possible solutions and testing them in practice. This enables us to ascertain whether we have solved the problem and can move on or, if not solved, to try and think again. Dewey considered the process applicable to all situations, although the problems, procedures, evidence and testing would depend on the context and the field of inquiry. 'Learning by doing' became his slogan. He regarded critique as a vital ingredient in the process and hence it is inevitably a social activity. The following example from *Better Mathematics* (Ahmed, 1987) attempts to explain an aspect of this process in practice.

> The 'statements' in the report have been used as generalisations to be refuted. For example, a Project member wrote about what happened when she used Statement 4.
>
> *Statement 4*
> *Mathematics is effectively learned only by experimenting, questioning, reflecting, discovering, inventing and discussing. Thus, for children, mathematics should be a kind of learning which requires a minimum of factual knowledge and a great deal of experience in dealing with situations using particular kinds of thinking skills.*
>
> I offered the teachers the statement and asked them to pinpoint any areas of disagreement. They had to provide concrete, personal examples to back up their point of view. No second-hand stories or myths were allowed.
>
> After small group discussion there was a feeling that the word 'only' in the statement was wrong. Many teachers gave their own schooling as examples. They said *they* had been taught without any experimentation in their grammar schools and yet had learned mathematics effectively.
>
> After some probing and discussion they decided that there was more to 'experimentation' and 'discovering' than 'scissors and paste'. They identified that this had often taken place outside class time, with friends, or on their own when experimentation and reflection were internalised.
>
> By the end of the session many wanted the word 'only' underlined and everyone had benefited from the discussion.
>
> (Ahmed, 1987, p. 9)

Maintaining the spirit of LAMP and RAMP

One of the conclusions of the RAMP report was that facts and skills taught in isolation from conceptual structures and general strategies can undermine pupils' confidence and competence. We signalled (Ahmed, 1995) that the implementation of the National Curriculum following the Education Reform Act (1988) 'had led teachers to concentrate mainly on planning and on improving teaching approaches, with second priority being given to the study of how pupils form elementary mathematical concepts' (p. 146). We also suggested that the rich research and development culture on teaching and learning mathematics in the UK, which was well known internationally, had lost its vigour since the introduction of the Act.

From our experience, one way of minimising the narrowing influence of an increasingly centralised curriculum on classroom practice is to utilise productively the partnership among the higher education sector, local education authorities (LEAs) and schools. It is important to bring about a clearer understanding of the ways in which teachers can continue to move from a cycle of aims/learning outcomes, content, teaching methods, assessment and evaluation to a more sophisticated research stance towards their own teaching. In particular, to consider a cycle which moves through purposes and emphases; knowledge and understanding of conceptual structures; rigour in choosing teaching and learning methods; critical appraisal, validation and communication. National initiatives can be used as a basis for enhancing these capabilities.

The National Numeracy Strategy (NNS) has provided teachers with training and support material to take on the challenge of providing all pupils with their 'entitlement' of mathematics education. In order for teachers to accrue most benefit from the resources and training provided, professional development will need to be considered as a long-term and continuous process. *Through engagement with projects and courses, teachers can continue to be involved in testing out in practice the implications of national initiatives.* We offer two examples in which we have attempted to maintain the principles of the LAMP and RAMP approaches to professional development within the NNS context, involving teachers as researchers.

Teachers as researchers

During the pilot phase of the NNS the authors, in conjunction with an LEA, carried out a small-scale study to help them, schools and teachers to develop a basis for ascertaining the effectiveness of the NNS compared to their existing practice for teaching numeracy. None of the schools were involved in the official pilot phase. In particular, the study wished to explore the implications of the following statement from *Numeracy Matters* (Reynolds, 1998a, para. 45):

> We believe that spreading what we have found to be the most effective methods of teaching numeracy to all primary classrooms will ensure that fewer children will fail to develop sound numeracy skills and go on to develop special educational needs.
>
> (p. 108)

In discussion with the LEA, ten primary schools were chosen in two clusters of five schools to work with two researchers. Each school nominated two classes for the study. The teaching and learning in one class was to follow the guidance and methodology prescribed by the National Numeracy project. In the other class the teaching followed the school's current practice. But both classes were to teach the same content. The research model chosen was participative, where both teachers and researchers took on interchangeable roles of teaching and researching. The teachers, as well as teaching, planning and assessing, were observing, reflecting and recording. The researchers were involved in teaching and being observed by teachers. This process created a climate of mutual confidence and helped establish trust among the participants. Joint meetings of participants from the ten schools were scheduled to help achieve consensus of interpretation of tasks and commonality of approach.

Observations and discussions

Achievement of pupil learning outcomes from individual lessons was not dependent on whether the teachers were following the approaches of the NNS or their normal classroom approach. There were examples of successes and failures equally in both groups. Some teachers who believed that they were rigidly following the exemplar lessons, in practice adopted a more responsive and flexible approach. Conversely, some of those who believed that they had the freedom to use a flexible approach appeared to be regimented and restrictive.

It was only when teachers had developed a wider appreciation of mathematics as a subject and confidence in thinking of themselves and their pupils as 'mathematical thinkers' that they were able to respond flexibly to a range of pupil responses and questions and lead them to the achievement of successful learning outcomes. For example, in one case an 'academically' well-qualified mathematics teacher, following the exemplar curriculum guidelines in teaching an area of probability, felt very vulnerable during open discussions with pupils in answering unanticipated questions. In contrast, an experienced non-mathematics-trained teacher who had developed a good grasp of important mathematical ideas, when faced with a similar situation, was at ease and confident in admitting that she did not immediately know the answer. She turned this into an excellent opportunity for joint learning. This exemplifies how teachers can cope with their own gaps in knowledge of the subject by using effective classroom strategies.

Teachers' responses to varying and changing pupil learning needs were a significant factor in influencing their pupils' learning outcomes. Teachers who were able to vary the pace as well as the mode of working with individuals and groups were more able to encourage pupils to sustain the work offered to them. For example, a teacher who had planned a free, exploratory session turned it into a fairly structured and instructional session on quickly assessing pupil needs.

Both the groups repeatedly remarked on the value of having a supportive critical friend in the classroom. It offered them an unparalleled opportunity for observing their own pupils more objectively, working as individuals, in groups and within the whole class. The subsequent discussions with the researchers helped to evaluate further their teaching approaches. The joint meetings were key for teachers to develop shared meaning and interpretation of mathematical content, teaching approaches and pupil learning outcomes.

The study reinforced for us that Reynolds' (1998b) assertion that 'teachers need a methodology that they can follow which has been proved to work . . .' (p. 20) can detract from teachers taking full responsibility for planning and implementing successful approaches in the classroom. Indeed, Reynolds' statement is as tricky as any assertion which purports to identify the needs of others, even pupils. There is a danger that the removal of this responsibility will, in the longer term, lead to teachers losing confidence both in their professional judgement and in their up-to-date knowledge and understanding of the mathematics they teach to their pupils.

In order for teachers to preserve the spirit which forms the basis of any curriculum change, and not just adopt the forms and rituals of the artefacts associated with the initiative, they need to be provided with opportunities where they can interact with colleagues as well as external 'experts'. Their involvement in informing and evaluating research is essential if the findings are to influence their practice.

Building on ongoing provision

We believe that, unlike mastering specific skills such as using ICT or improving knowledge of mathematical topics, the craft of teaching cannot be developed in isolation. Articulating beliefs and practice and seeking confirmation for successful and unsuccessful experiences are essential. An example of how we are currently attempting to achieve this is described below.

In conjunction with neighbouring education authorities, we have been able to offer teachers who have undertaken numeracy training courses an opportunity to build upon and follow up areas of interest to themselves and/or their schools. Teachers commit to undertake a small-scale project as well as attend a specified number of twilight sessions. Some groups are able to attend a whole day workshop, often on Saturdays. During the initial twilight sessions, teachers are offered stimuli in the form of mathematical activities and/or issues concerned with the learning and teaching of mathematics. Working with colleagues on these, and reflecting on their numeracy training, helps to sharpen their intended focus. The twilight sessions and Saturday workshops, as well as e-mail contact with teachers and ourselves, enable participants to refine their projects and find relevant literature and resources to support their study. Observation of specific pupils' learning of mathematics must be integral to the study. Figure 1 shows the framework that is provided to help teachers to write their project report.

Guidelines for the journal and oral presentation

What, why, when, how . . .

1. Identify an area of interest either arising out of the Numeracy Training or from your own experience.
2. Explain why the chosen area is of particular interest to you and your school. You may need to give some background and context of yourself and your class/school.
3. How did you follow up this area? Describe your experience/experiment.
4. What did you find out? Provide evidence and give examples, if appropriate, of pupils'/teachers' responses.
5. What did you learn as a result of the work? How would you do it again if you had the opportunity?
6. What recommendations will you make to others?
7. Make reference to resources which supported you, for example, books, articles, websites, people, and explain how.

Figure 1. Framework for the project report

At the end of the year, teachers are also asked to make a 15-minute presentation to colleagues as well as present a written study/report of approximately 4,000 words which will be of help to themselves and/or their schools. Extracts from two such reports are shown below.

Extracts from teachers' notes

Teacher A

During my work in schools over the last seven years, I have observed a significant range of differences in the attitudes, abilities and learning methods of pupils in all areas of the curriculum, therefore I believe that this area would benefit from further enquiry in order to ascertain explanations for pupil performance that could undoubtedly be of notable relevance to the teaching of mathematics. If, as I am suggesting, attitudes do correlate with attainment, then I propose that teachers can motivate children's attitudes, thereby positively affecting their attainment.

I hope to provide evidence, through this small, class-based study, that will support this statement.

This research study has encouraged me to become consciously aware of my attitude to maths teaching and learning and the attitude that I portray to the children. Like parents, I will be a valuable role model for pupils and they may often adopt my attitudes until they have formed their own. Recognising the effects of negative attitudes and the benefits of positive ones on attainment, I hope to be able to use them to positively develop the potential of my pupils, schemes of work, and colleagues. I had previously recognised the importance of the methodology that I had used, however this study has impressed upon me that methodology should not be compromised, given the detrimental effect that it can have upon the children's attitudes and attainments.

I have thoroughly enjoyed this research and have come away with many new skills and ideas that will be of great value in my teaching and future class-based studies. My teaching and role as subject coordinator will be affected by the implications of these findings. It has made me realise that a teacher's personal interest in promoting a particular area of the curriculum has a great part to play on pupils' reactions and results in that area. Effectiveness of methodology in the promotion of positive attitudes relies upon a significant factor – variety. If the variety of stimulus is removed, one single method will lose its effectiveness and, consequently, break the chain reaction.

Teacher B

My first steps as a researcher
My first steps as a researcher complete, I now needed to collate all my findings. 'Observing' is inextricably interwoven with where I am at a particular time. I make decisions about what I will observe and these observations relate to where I am now. I see myself stumbling through those first steps and yet learning at every stage. Oh, if only I was able to retrace them, but now with so much learnt and so much more to do I am able to reflect, pace myself and move forward.

What was pertinent at the beginning of my study has evolved from simple interest about my own class to a methodology for research by all staff in the school for self-evaluation.

I now see that my initial question, 'Is it a myth that my class only learn when I am with them?' has now been answered. I have also learnt that teachers have to be confident in themselves and in their own mathematics to allow children to explore for themselves. Similarly the children gain considerably more if they are to have that inner confidence in their own abilities. This was particularly evident with the children I observed, and was reinforced by the teachers' responses to the discussion paper.

Advice for others

It is very clear that although I have had many varied experiences in my chosen career I have until now had no experience as a researcher, so what valuable insight am I qualified or able to give? Quite simply that I am now, from my own personal experience, able to say that it is extremely beneficial for all teachers to return to the position of learner with a new, clearly defined focus. For myself, that was to begin to develop the skills of a researcher.

Within those skills, I have gained from reading a variety of papers by experienced researchers and by teachers in a similar position to myself. I believe that by using their experiences one can focus on the most appropriate research skills to develop for the investigation. However, it is only by experiencing the pitfalls and successes for oneself that one can truly learn. One has to take into account previous personal experiences and the situation within the school where the research is to take place, all of which are different for every individual.

I can only reiterate that I believe the experiences I have had to create this report should be part of all teachers' ongoing professional development – head teachers, senior staff and class teachers alike.

An invitation

In 1987 we made eight recommendations concerned with the professional development of teachers (Ahmed, 1987). We invite the readers to challenge the assumptions and examine to what extent these recommendations (below) can contribute to alleviating the problems associated with the teaching and learning of mathematics to low attaining pupils outlined at the beginning of this chapter.

Recommendations

1. Effective change will take time and effort. Ways of making time available for teachers to work together need to be explored urgently as part of a regular pattern of in-service provision. However, to provide time without paying adequate attention to the quality of in-service experience is of no value.

2. In-service providers must act as 'catalysts' in order to ensure that this regular professional development is stimulated and facilitated. Teachers must be actively involved in this process in order to develop their confidence, motivation, autonomy and professionalism both in providing for their pupils' needs and in terms of their own mathematics.

3. This professional development must be recognised as a long-term and continuous process. Short cuts are a false economy.

4. In this chapter the Project has identified elements which must form essential parts of teachers' professional development. They have implications for all those involved with in-service provision.

5. If changes in teachers' behaviour are to be facilitated, teachers must be involved in challenging and critically examining their own beliefs.

6. In-service providers must believe that teachers are capable of developing in the ways we have indicated. Hence, they too must be involved in challenging and critically examining their own beliefs.

7. It is essential to recognise that expertise lies in teachers' own experiences. This is fundamental to the developmental process.

8. In-service providers must not be tempted to smooth over the uncertainties and challenges that are an inherent and essential part of teacher development. The ability to face and use dilemmas productively should be highly valued as an objective.

(Ahmed, 1987, p. 38)

References

AHMED, A. (Project Director) (1987) *Better Mathematics*. LAMP Report. London: HMSO.

AHMED, A. (1995) Mathematics – a tale of three worlds? *Teaching Mathematics and its Application*, 14(4).

AHMED, A. and WILLIAMS, H. (1992) *Raising Achievement in Mathematics Project*. RAMP Report. West Sussex: ChIHE/HMSO.

BENNETT, A. and WILLIAMS, H. (1992) What will happen if? An active approach to mathematics teaching. In T. Booth, W. Swann, M. Masterson and P. Potts (eds), *Curricula for Diversity in Education*. London: Routledge/Open University.

COCKCROFT, W. H. (Chair) (1982) *Mathematics Counts: Report of the Committee of Enquiry*. London: HMSO.

DES (1985) *Mathematics from 5 to 16: Curriculum matters 3*. London: HMSO.

DfEE (1998) *The Implementation of the National Numeracy Strategy – The Final Report of the Numeracy Task Force*. London: DfEE.

DfES (2002) *Qualifying to Teach: Professional Standards for Qualified Teacher Status and Requirements for Initial Teacher Training*. London: DfES/TTA.

HESSE, H. (1973) *Siddhartha*. Reading: Picador.

McCULLOCH, G. and McCAIG, C. (2002) Reinventing the past: The case of the English tradition of education. *British Journal of Educational Studies*, 50(2), 238–53.

MAGEE, B. (1998) *The Story of Philosophy*. London: Dorling Kindersley.

MOORE, J. and MORRISON, N. (1998) *Someone Else's Problem? Teacher Development to Meet Special Educational Needs*. London: Falmer Press.

REYNOLDS, D. (Chair) (1998a) *Numeracy Matters – the preliminary report of the numeracy task force*. London: DfEE.

REYNOLDS, D. (1998b) Teachers should be more like technicians. Report of the third TES Keele lecture. *Times Educational Supplement*, 17/7/98.

CHAPTER 2

Low attaining students can think mathematically

ANNE WATSON

Pupils who do well in school mathematics appear to succeed in a variety of ways which can be loosely grouped around two descriptions. First, there are those who easily recall and use rules, techniques and procedures and pass examinations with relative ease so long as the questions are of familiar kinds requiring the accurate application of procedural knowledge. Then there are those who develop complex ways of interacting with mathematical text and thinking about the concepts and ideas thus encountered. These students can succeed in familiar and unfamiliar situations.

What about failure? Failure in mathematics, like failure in other school subjects, can be a result of affective issues, disrupted education and specific learning difficulties. Failure in mathematics can also be due to lack of development in the ways of thinking about mathematics which come naturally to those who, hence, succeed. Often, however, support for weaker students focuses on rules, techniques and procedures – sometimes called the 'basics' of mathematics. Learners are encouraged to be like the first type described in the paragraph above, rather than the second. Emphasis might be on recall and application, yet these learners have not remembered and may not recognise situations as familiar ones in which to apply their knowledge. Little emphasis is generally given to helping them develop ways of thinking which may improve future learning. Little help is given them to construct complex understanding which provides the context for recall and application of procedures. Little attention is given to building on pupils' existing understandings and mental images. Currently, the materials provided to schools for those 'falling behind' largely fit this description (that is, rules, techniques and procedures), though of course they may be imaginatively used by teachers to create more challenging lessons.

Mathematics support which is based on performance of simple skills is often given in conjunction with attention to affective matters. For instance, work can be contextualised into familiar contexts; practical applications, such as planning a party, might be used to provide a motivation to do some budgeting and measuring exercises; *ad hoc* mathematical methods might be used to do some shopping for the school; mathematics might be hidden in a 'fun' context for which prizes might be given, and so on.

Of course, such approaches to mathematics can benefit low attaining students hugely, so long as the mathematics being learnt is helping them to make progress in the cognitive domain; but using *low* level mathematics in context, while building social confidence, might contribute little to future learning.

As a consequence of my own recent experiences teaching Year 9 low attaining students for one term in a nearby school I began to feel that there is much to be written about how to support such students in the development of mathematical thinking (Watson, 2000). It is particularly clear that non-specialist teachers and assistants, whose own experience of mathematics might be of rules, techniques and procedures (with the associated fears or failures), cannot automatically see ways in which the support they ably offer in other subjects can be given in mathematics. The temptation is to resort to demonstrating how to do things rather than using adult–pupil interactions which allow more sophisticated knowledge and ways of thinking to develop.

In this chapter I will give some examples of students from this class showing characteristics of mathematical thinking often associated with high achieving students. These suggest that whatever is hampering their mathematical attainment is *not* an inability to think in the ways which enable others to succeed.

Recent research on the brain describes how natural brain functions and human behaviour form the foundations of mathematical thinking (for example, Butterworth, 1999; Dehaene, 1997; Lakoff and Nunez, 2000). The implication is that abilities to think mathematically and understand mathematical concepts are adaptations of our natural brain and bodily activities, given elementary inborn propensities to recognise and compare small numbers. If this is true, then those who are better at mathematics than others must be better at learning from mathematical experiences, rather than have innate superior abilities. The national emphasis in the UK on raising standards has led to higher achievement for some students, according to current measures. This shows that teaching *can* make a difference to achievement when guided by higher expectations. But emphasis on raising the achievements of those who are slightly below the target standards often ignores those who are well below those levels. Of course, we have to take the evidence of rising standards with a slight dose of scepticism . . . could it be that all we are seeing is the improved ability of teachers to 'teach to the tests'? But whatever is the reason for rising national test results, there are still many who are not achieving.

I am going to apply a broader meaning to 'achievement' than just test results. The recent PISA 2000 results show that UK 15-year-olds (who were not affected by current numeracy practices) were among the highest achieving internationally in a broad-based mathematics test which included reasoning skills, approaches to unfamiliar situations and problem-solving as well as the more usual international test items. But there were still some who did very poorly. It is these students, and this broad description of achievement, which I wish to address.

Some clear barriers to learning

For some students there are clear barriers to mathematical learning about which we can be much more specific than merely referring to poor concentration, emotional and social difficulties and so on. For instance, the ability to choose appropriate and efficient strategies, and to adapt them if necessary, is seen as a characteristic of high achieving mathematicians (Krutetskii, 1976). In Harding's (2000) detailed examination of students' take-up of mental arithmetic strategies she found that a few students, even after close one-to-one teaching, were unable to develop a repertoire of strategies. The strategy they used changed as the project succeeded, but they changed from *always* doing calculations one way to *always* doing them another. They seemed to find being offered alternatives confusing. These students appeared to be unable to choose strategies, in spite of careful personal teaching. This is an example of what I mean by a 'clear barrier to mathematical learning'.

In the study I am about to describe there was one adolescent student out of 11 in the class who showed no evidence at all of mathematical thinking processes. In a one-to-one interview he was asked to 'double' nine in three different contexts during half-an-hour. Each time he used a 'count all' strategy afresh; he was unable to recall that he had already done the calculation, or to recall whether the answer he reached was correct or not. His short-term memory problems (or it could have been an inability to abstract a cardinal understanding of number) were a 'clear barrier to mathematical learning'.

Another example of a clear barrier to learning is given by Tomkys (2001), who tells of a young student whose performance in subtraction calculations was correct until the end, when she always subtracted one from the units as a final operation. In spite of being able to spend several hours in one-to-one teaching, the teacher was unable to locate the source of this error, supposing in the end that it was a misapplication of a rule which might sometimes apply correctly to the 'tens' column. It is a common experience that some students become fixated on applying inappropriate rules. Even when the student successfully demonstrated subtraction with apparatus, and followed or even initiated correct chains of reasoning with the teacher, she still subtracted one after all other work had been done. It was several weeks before the student was able to adapt this incorrect strategy. This story shows that identification of a 'clear barrier to mathematical learning' can lead to focused, effective teaching . . . although it might take some time to achieve anything. Ann Dowker in Chapter 3 gives more examples of such barriers.

I have given three examples of barriers to learning: inability to cope with choice; inability to give up a 'known' rule; and inability to remember very recent results, or to shift from counting to a cardinal concept of number (for similar cases, see Butterworth, 1999). Any teacher will have similar stories about students from whom they gain very detailed knowledge of specific barriers to learning; but it is also worth reporting that *most* students in Harding's study, rather than just the highest achieving, *did* exhibit the complex strategy-choosing behaviour described by Krutetskii. It seems to be true that explicit teaching of useful ways to think can improve the attainment of many. The CAME project, reported in this book by Mundher Adhami (Chapter 13), and its predecessor in science teaching, the CASE project (Adey and Shayer, 1994), found that students who had been encouraged to think enquiringly in science or mathematics did better in a range of other unrelated subjects than a comparative group who had not had the same experiences. These studies lead me to ask: what ways of thinking are employed by successful mathematical learners, and does it help to teach these explicitly to low attaining students?

A proficiency approach to mathematical thinking

The questions I have posed so far assume a deficit model of the mathematical thinking skills of low attaining students. However, Harries' work reported in this book (Chapter 8), suggests a different approach. He placed students in a situation in which they could leave a trace of their thinking, showing clearly how they completed a mathematical drawing task. Rather than consider teaching such students to act out the characteristics of successful mathematicians, we could continue from Harries' work and look at their proficiencies rather than their deficiencies. What kinds of thinking, which might lead to higher attainment in mathematics, are manifested in the work of low attaining students? To recognise some of these, and work for their enhancement, avoids the temptation to reduce complex ways of thinking to lists of simplified heuristics which are then performed as algorithms, rather than experienced as deeply creative processes.

Harries found evidence that most students were able to transcend a purely manipulative approach through seeing objects they had made at one stage of their work as tools to use in the next stage. These types of shift characterise the genesis of mathematics, as generations of mathematicians developed the subject as we know it today. For example, addition develops from getting an answer by *enumerating* the combined contents of two sets, through an appreciation of *cardinality*, to using known *number bonds as tools* for harder addition sums. This shift is inherent in the structure of mathematics, so it is also a useful shift for a learner to make.

That Harries found such a shift being made spontaneously by low attaining students suggests that there might be other forms of mathematical thinking which have been characterised as features of the work of high achieving students, but which all *can* do. For some reason these forms may not have been harnessed in the teaching they have received, or their response to it. I do not want here to discuss reasons why this harnessing has not happened, but to point to some other types of mathematical thinking which I have found some lower attaining students to be using, or to be able to use.

The study

The intake of the school in which I worked was skewed towards lower-than-average attainment levels, and this particular class contained about 11 regular attenders (rather fewer than were on roll) who had a variety of behavioural problems, language differences, patchy school histories and learning difficulties. There would usually be one or two support assistants in addition to the usual teacher. I had arranged to observe one double lesson each week with the intention of finding out how students would respond to particular kinds of questioning and prompting within their normal lessons. In the event, many factors typical of school life prevented the study proceeding as planned and I became a teacher or support assistant as well as an observer and interviewer. Nevertheless, I was able to build up a substantial record of classroom incidents in which students showed that they could make shifts, either independently or with suitable prompts, which led them into forms of mathematical thought beyond the superficial features of the given task. Here I shall discuss two examples.

An example of flexible use of representation

Near the end of a lesson in which students had been working with fractions I drew some identical squares on the chalkboard and asked students to come and indicate how to quarter the squares (Figure 1). The first offering was a drawing of the obvious vertical and horizontal lines; the next was the two diagonals; the third, after a short wait, was a dissection using three vertical lines to give four congruent strips. So far students had interpreted the task as producing four congruent shapes and there had been a sense among those who came to the board of taking responsibility for getting the usual examples done. After waiting in silence a while I drew a version which had two 'strip' quarters and two 'square' quarters. There was a pause while they considered what I had done. I asked them to vote on whether they believed I had cut the square into quarters or not. I was trying to encourage them to shift from seeing fractions as congruent shapes to seeing fractions as quantities – in this case making a link with area. Some of them were able to do this, offering area as the way to 'see' it. One student saw that further cutting and rearranging of the pieces would allow you to see that they were equal in area. After this I paused and waited to see if anyone would offer other ideas. One student offered the same dissection rotated through a right angle. Then Darren drew a version with three slanting lines, including one diagonal.

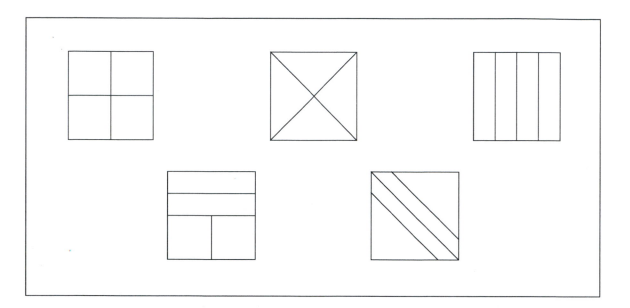

Figure 1. Examples of how students attempted to divide squares into quarters

Because these students are labelled 'low attainers' it is tempting to assume that he was wrong; that he had not understood that the four pieces had to be equal in area. Giving up congruence as a criterion *may* have suggested that one could give up equality of any kind. He could also have been trying to extend the idea of cutting diagonally by mixing it with parallel cuts. This seems likely, given how the diagonal idea had not yet been developed further. I asked him if he was sure about where his lines should go. He said he was not, and that he did not know where to put them 'to make each half into halves'. Of course, my question 'Are you sure?' may have given him the clue to answer 'No', but his voluntary elaboration of the negative answer revealed that he knew more; he had realised that deciding where to put the lines was hard but that there ought to be a solution. Another student, the one who had suggested rearranging pieces before, said 'You can cut them up and move them around' but could not show us how to do that. The end of the lesson came and I was unable to pursue this further.

It is hard to say exactly what was going on for individuals in this story. Most of them were able to shift from seeing fractions as congruent parts to fractions as something about equal areas, that is, they were able to use the spatial representation in a different way, as a result of being offered the idea and asked to work with it. A few had taken this further and made a definite link with area. One had been prepared to abandon the square and move shapes around, so that demonstrating equality was more important than retaining the original shape. No one had completely abandoned the notion of symmetry playing a role in this. It seemed as if most of the students were able to adapt their interpretations of a very familiar representation, but this happened to varying extents. I was struck that they were able to make such shifts, given the opportunity to do so.

Symbolisation can create difficulties for learners in mathematics. All truly mathematical ideas are necessarily abstract and we only have access to them through the way they are represented on the page or with materials capable of manipulation. It follows, then, that learners whose understanding of an underlying concept can be independent of a particular representation of it are in a better position to extend their understanding outside the confines of one representation, or to recognise a familiar concept in unfamiliar clothes. Dreyfus (1991) therefore points to flexible use of representations as a useful advanced skill in working with mathematics. Here were students who were, to various degrees, willing to use representations flexibly . . . yet they were not 'advanced'.

An example of abstraction

Almira had been given a list of coordinates of points in the positive quadrant. The task was to plot them all on a coordinate grid and join them up in the order given to make a picture. The finished picture was thus an in-built self-checking device. When I looked at her work she had drawn in a number of unconnected lines, rather than systematically going from point to point in the order offered (Figure 2). On closer inspection it was clear that she had gone through the list of points and found all adjacent pairs which were of the form (a, b) with (a + 1, b − 1) and had entered those points and drawn the associated vector (1, −1). In other words, she had focused on the relationships between the points rather than the points themselves, and selected all those for which the relationship was the same. In drawing these in she had to use the actual positions of the points, but had created for herself a higher level task involving identifying relationships, classifying them, and performing all those of the same type at once. In conversation with her I found out that she had done this to make the task 'more interesting' and had thought it more efficient. In fact, she was having to do deeper thinking and make more passes through the data in order to complete the drawing, so she could be said to be doing *more* work, but her interest was in the relationships and not the finished drawing. Here was a low attaining student who had voluntarily made the task more abstract and complex by shifting her focus from the coordinates to the relationships between objects, using coordinates as a tool to get her started and using the drawn lines themselves conceptually. In a sense she had invented the concept of 'vector' (qualities which, in two dimensions, can be represented by lines which have a given length and direction) for herself. This shift would not be apparent in the finished drawing. Without a record of how the drawing was constructed, such as Harries' students were able to produce, or my fortuitous observation, Almira's thinking about the task may not have been recognised.

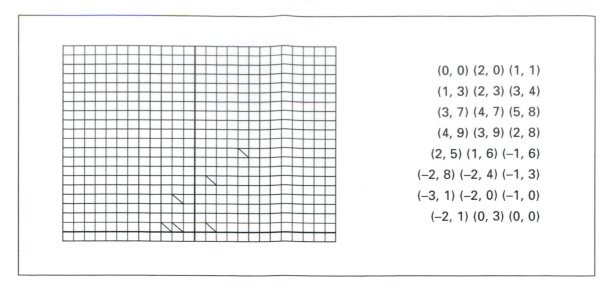

(0, 0) (2, 0) (1, 1)
(1, 3) (2, 3) (3, 4)
(3, 7) (4, 7) (5, 8)
(4, 9) (3, 9) (2, 8)
(2, 5) (1, 6) (–1, 6)
(–2, 8) (–2, 4) (–1, 3)
(–3, 1) (–2, 0) (–1, 0)
(–2, 1) (0, 3) (0, 0)

Figure 2. Almira's work on the coordinate grid

Almira demonstrated a deliberate shift from process to concept. To extend an earlier example, addition develops from being the process of combined enumeration to being seen as only one of many ways of combining two or more numbers – an example of the concept of binary operation. Such ability to combine the roles of process and concept has been described as a component of advanced mathematical thinking (Tall, 1991, p. 254). Equating, for example, leads us to understand equations; then having equations as a tool lets us use them in complex situations and treat them as objects in their own right, not just as relationships between other objects. Thus 'equating' can be a technical skill, a concept, or an abstraction depending on how it is used and how it is seen by the learner. In Almira's work, she turns the process of joining dots into a vector concept, and then works with similarities and differences within this new-for-her concept.

Issues for teachers

Harries points to the work of Krutetskii (1976), who characterised the thinking of successful Russian mathematics students as a possible source of information on ways to think. Other sources of knowledge about mathematical thinking would be: Polya (1962) and Schoenfeld (1985), who describe problem-solving heuristics; Mason, Burton and Stacey (1982), who talk more generally about ways to work with mathematics, both solving problems and exploring new ideas; and Dubinsky (1991), who discusses the Piagetian process of reflective abstraction as a component of advanced mathematical thinking. None of these writers suggests that explicit teaching can help others think in these ways; nevertheless the publication of their ideas suggests an implicit theoretical belief that identifying, naming and disseminating such descriptions makes them available for wider use. Teachers, however, often adopt different teaching styles for different teaching groups (see Ollerton, Chapter 14). This suggests a *professional* belief that it is not appropriate to expect lower achieving students to approach topics in the same way that others might. High achieving students might be expected to grasp abstract concepts quickly, manipulate and explore them, deal with alternatives, find their way through complexities, and so on. By contrast, less successful students are seen to need more structured, step-by-step approaches, mathematics presented in practical, contextualised or 'fun' forms, and the practice of simple algorithms.

But there is no standard recipe for mathematical success. Dahl (2000) found that successful Year 13 students had a variety of different ways of working on new mathematics. There was not even commonality about how they worked: whether by accepting the general statements of others and manifesting them through specific examples, or by using specific examples to help them understand generalities for themselves. There were also various ways of using intuition and shortcuts in their work. If there is no universal recipe for mathematical thinking, and an extant belief that low attaining students must think in lower level ways, what can teachers do to discover, exploit and develop the abstract thinking which might be taking place?

In Harries' work, a situation had been created in which traces of thinking could be 'read' by the teacher, but the activity itself structured the opportunity given to learners to make the shifts he sought. In Darren's case, the task had been chosen to give an opportunity to go beyond the usual responses; the teacher waited for a while and then gave a clue that other things were possible; creative responses were expected and, eventually, one was given. In Almira's case, the activity offered the opportunity to approach the task in a variety of ways, from mundane to abstract. Once her approach had been seen and recognised by a teacher who may not already have seen the possibilities, questions and prompts could be devised for other learners to help them make the same shift. In this case, I proceeded to ask other students, 'What is the same about these two lines? Can you see patterns in the numbers for these two lines?' and so on. By doing this, I found that nearly all the class could make a similar shift, given the prompting and the chance to do so.

So there are several questions which arise for teachers of low attaining students in mathematics. Is it possible to structure work so that complex mathematical thinking is encouraged and noticed, even in simple mathematical situations? Could teachers trust more such students to think in mathematically sophisticated ways, even in simple situations? How can teachers recognise sophisticated approaches when they are being used, then value them by making them explicit for others?

References

ADEY, P. and SHAYER, M. (1994) *Really Raising Standards: Cognitive intervention and academic achievement*. London: Routledge.

BUTTERWORTH, B. (1999) *The Mathematical Brain*. London: Macmillan.

DAHL, B. (2000) *A case study of high-achieving pupils of mathematics: how the psychology of learning mathematics relates to their reported learning experiences*. Unpublished M.Sc. dissertation, University of Oxford.

DEHAENE, S. (1997) *The Number Sense: How the mind creates mathematics*. London: Allen Lane.

DREYFUS, T. (1991) Advanced mathematical thinking processes. In D. Tall (ed.), *Advanced Mathematical Thinking*. Dordrecht: Kluwer.

DUBINSKY, E. (1991) Reflective abstraction in advanced mathematical thinking. In D. Tall (ed.), *Advanced Mathematical Thinking*. Dordrecht: Kluwer.

HARDING, B. (2000) *The development of mental strategies in children of differing abilities*. Unpublished M.Sc. dissertation, Manchester Metropolitan University.

KRUTETSKII, V. A. (1976) (trans. J. Teller), J. Kilpatrick and I. Wirszup (eds), *The Psychology of Mathematical Abilities in School Children*. Chicago: University Chicago Press.

LAKOFF, G. and NUNEZ, R. E. (2000) *Where Mathematics Comes From*. New York: Basic Books.

MASON, J., BURTON, L. and STACEY, K. (1982) *Thinking Mathematically*. London: Addison Wesley.

PISA 2000. Online at http://www.pisa.oecd.org

POLYA, G. (1962) *Mathematical Discovery: On understanding, learning, and teaching problem solving.* New York: Wiley.

SCHOENFELD, A. (1985) *Mathematical Problem Solving.* San Diego, CA: Academic Press.

TALL, D. (ed.) (1991) *Advanced Mathematical Thinking.* Dordrecht: Kluwer.

TOMKYS, S. (2000) Personal communication.

WATSON, A. (2000) Going across the grain: mathematical generalisations in a group of low attaining students. *Nordic Studies in Mathematics Education,* 8(1), 7–20.

Individuals

The five chapters in this section involve the idea of looking closely at how individual learners respond to specific aspects of mathematics. They are written from different perspectives – that of teacher, LSA and researcher – and involve learners in the infant, junior and secondary age range. All seek to find out about and help students who appear to have difficulty with mathematics.

In Chapter 3 Ann Dowker discusses a pilot 'numeracy recovery' scheme for six- and seven-year-old children with numeracy difficulties. The chapter takes the view that children are rarely uniformly weak on all aspects of arithmetic, but may have difficulties with particular components. The author offers advice about what to look for when assessing children who appear to find arithmetic difficult and makes suggestions for focused intervention. The chapter ends on an optimistic note, supporting the idea that children are highly responsive to such intervention. In Chapter 4 Tony Harries, Ruth Barrington and Cathy Hamilton describe a study carried out as part of an INSET programme with teachers of seven- to eleven-year-olds. This study aimed to explore ways in which pupils explained their approaches to addition and subtraction calculations, and to explore pupils' images of numbers. The authors make the point that assessment of low attaining pupils should not just be about error analysis, but should also include a consideration of explanations given by pupils, which can give important information about their thinking.

In Chapter 5 Jenny Houssart looks at one nine-year-old girl, Julie, who has difficulties with harder aspects of counting. The author adopted a role similar to that of an LSA. She shows how a picture of an individual can be built up by watching his/her response to a range of ordinary classroom tasks, and that LSAs are in a strong position to obtain detailed information about children's strengths and difficulties in mathematics. The implications of this are considered. Chapter 6 also looks closely at one pupil, John, a 14-year-old student in a mixed-ability mathematics class who is described as having 'moderate learning difficulties'. Written from the perspective of John's teacher, Mike Ollerton gives examples of the work carried out by John on Pythagoras' theorem. There is also a discussion of issues applicable to learners at all levels, for example the construction of short and medium term plans which take into account differences in learning. Mike asserts that responding to John within a mixed-ability environment helped him become a more effective teacher for all students. Chapter 7 looks at particular incidents drawn from classrooms where the children had low levels of attainment in mathematics and some also had potentially challenging behaviour. The incidents all involve the apparent refusal of a child to do a task, and the focus is on the nature of the task in question. Jenny Houssart presents possible explanations for children's behaviour, related to the mathematics task structure.

The chapters in this section acknowledge the complexity of learning and teaching, but suggest that by looking closely at individuals learning mathematics we are likely to gain understanding about how they may be helped. An added bonus is that in looking at this closely we are likely to see positive features of children's work alongside their difficulties.

CHAPTER 3

Numeracy recovery: a pilot scheme for early intervention with young children with numeracy difficulties

ANN DOWKER

Specific difficulties in arithmetic have rarely received the same attention as specific difficulties in reading and writing; but it is likely that a higher proportion of adults experience persistent numeracy difficulties than persistent literacy difficulties.

Counting and basic number concepts appear to be universal across cultures and to develop early, as pointed out, for example, by Dehaene (1997) and Butterworth (1999). However, numerous studies (for example the Basic Skills Agency, 1997) demonstrate that a significant number of adults experience difficulties with arithmetic and, for instance, find it difficult to carry out arithmetical tasks of a type that are important in daily life, and have negative emotional reactions to arithmetic. According to ALBSU (1992), a high proportion of adults with severe numeracy difficulties had already shown signs of arithmetical difficulties in the early school years.

In the area of reading skills, there has already been considerable emphasis on early identification of individual patterns of strengths and weaknesses, and their use in compensatory education for 'backward' readers; for example, the Reading Recovery programme set up by Clay (1985) and reviewed and evaluated by Sylva and Hurry (1995). However, there had been, especially until recently, little comparable work in the field of mathematical development and mathematics education, though the need for individualised diagnosis and remediation of arithmetical difficulties has been recognised by some people for many years, for example Williams and Whitaker (1937) and Weaver (1954).

In the last few years there has been some increase in provision of programmes aimed at overcoming mathematical difficulties. These include: the overall increased focus on mathematics for all children reflected in the Numeracy Strategy; a few preschool intervention programmes targeted at high-risk groups with the aim of preventing later difficulties (for example, those set up by Griffin, Case and Siegler, 1994 and by Ginsburg, Balfanz and Greenes, 1999); and a few individualised and intensive programmes targeted at children who are already having difficulties (notably, the Mathematics Recovery programme devised by Wright, Martland and Stafford, 2000). But there is still very little compared to the relatively wide variety of programmes available for poor readers. In particular, there has been very little of an individualised, but relatively non-intensive, nature.

Some of my previous research (Dowker, 1995; 1998) has suggested that specific arithmetical weaknesses are quite common, and are often restricted to particular components of arithmetic, for example: written symbolism; memory for number facts; estimation. These findings have led to consideration of the desirability of a Numeracy

Recovery scheme for assessing and ameliorating children's difficulties with specific areas of arithmetic in the early primary school years, before they have developed inappropriate arithmetical strategies based on fundamental misunderstandings and/or developed negative or even phobic reactions to arithmetic.

While many forms of extra one-to-one teaching are likely to be helpful to children with difficulties, techniques that are targeted toward an individual child's specific weaknesses would seem likely to be most effective.

The Numeracy Recovery project and the distinctive principles behind it

Such a Numeracy Recovery scheme, funded by the Esmée Fairbairn Charitable Trust, is being piloted with six- and seven-year-olds (mostly Year 2) in some first schools in Oxford. The scheme involves working with children who have been identified by their teachers as having problems with arithmetic.

The distinctive characteristics of the intervention scheme are as follows:

1. It is based on a componential view of arithmetical ability

Arithmetic is seen not as a unitary ability, but as composed of multiple components, themselves divisible into many subcomponents. Each of these components shows continuous variation within the population, from extreme talent to extreme deficit. Such components include: basic number knowledge; memory for arithmetical facts; the understanding of concepts; and the ability to follow procedures. Each of these components has, in turn, a number of subcomponents:

- Number knowledge involves the ability to recognise numbers in different forms (numerals, number words, and concrete quantities) and to place them in order.
- Factual knowledge involves memory for different categories of facts (e.g. addition, multiplication, subtraction, division).
- Conceptual understanding involves, for example, understanding of the properties of and relationships between arithmetical operations; also the ability to use them in the derivation of unknown arithmetical facts, especially where standard calculation procedures are also unknown, or are cumbersome and time-consuming. Unknown fact derivation includes both the derivation of new exact arithmetical answers from known facts by means of arithmetical principles such as commutativity and associativity (as discussed by Baroody, Ginsburg and Waxman, 1983), and the derivation of approximate answers, that is, estimation (reviewed by Sowder, 1992). Another aspect of conceptual knowledge is the semantic understanding of an arithmetical word problem or real-world arithmetical problem, and the ability to select the arithmetical operations and strategies appropriate to the problem in question (DeCorte and Verschaffel, 1987).

The latter subcomponent interacts with procedural knowledge which involves, for example: memory for learned procedures; ability to carry them out in an appropriate sequence without losing track; and, in the case of written calculation, correct spatial alignment of numerals.

Moreover, procedural knowledge, and possibly other components, may vary with the format of presentation (auditory versus visual; concrete versus numerical) and, indeed, Hughes (1986) has pointed out that one important subcomponent of arithmetical ability may be the ability to translate from one format to another.

Though the different components often correlate with one another, weaknesses in any one of them can occur relatively independently of weaknesses in the others. Weaknesses in even one component can ultimately take their toll on performance in other components – partly because difficulty with one component may increase the risk of the child relying exclusively on another component and failing to perceive and use relationships between different arithmetical processes and problems – and partly because when children fail at certain tasks they may come to perceive themselves as 'no good at maths' and develop a negative attitude to the subject. However, the components described here are not seen as a hierarchy. A child may perform well at an apparently difficult task (for example, word problem-solving) while performing poorly at an apparently easier component (for example, remembering the counting word sequence). Though certain specific components may frequently form the basis for learning other specific components, they need not always be prerequisites. Denvir and Brown (1986), Dowker (1998) and others have suggested that it is not possible to establish a strict hierarchy whereby any one component invariably precedes another component. There are probably a few very basic components that *do* precede and form a basis for the later development of other components. As Butterworth (1999) has pointed out, these basic components include recognition of quantities up to three; they may also include understanding the earliest developing counting principles as discussed, for example, by Greeno, Riley and Gelman (1984). However, such components will usually be fully developed in typically developing six-year-old children, even those who are weak at numeracy, and therefore are not relevant to intervention with most such children.

2. The scheme involves close collaboration between the researcher and the classroom teachers

The teachers have been involved at all levels: in preliminary discussions with the researcher to help to establish the areas with which children most frequently experience difficulty and which are therefore important to address in an intervention programme; in selecting the children most likely to benefit from intervention; and in actually carrying out the intervention work. This collaboration has a number of important benefits:

- The researcher is aided in making an informed selection of the components which most frequently create problems for children in the mathematics classroom.
- The intervention is carried out in the context in which the children are receiving the majority of their mathematics instruction. This reduces the risk of children failing to transfer their knowledge gains from the intervention context to the everyday educational context.
- The teachers can transfer the intervention techniques, and the understanding that the individualised work gives them of children's individual strengths and deficits, to classroom work with the same children and sometimes other children.
- The children's arithmetical strengths and weaknesses are observed from several perspectives: standardised test performance; performance on the different components during the individualised assessments; their performance during the

training sessions; and their performance in the classroom situation. Through collaboration between teachers and the researcher, a more detailed, accurate and valid picture of these strengths and weaknesses can be built up than if the children were only observed from one or two of these perspectives.

3. Although the project is individualised, it is relatively non-intensive, making it easier to carry out in schools which are under the type of administrative pressure common in schools nowadays

Children in the programme receive about half an hour of intervention a week. While some children would undoubtedly benefit from more intensive intervention programmes if these were practically possible, it is thought that a significant number need just a relatively small amount of individualised and targeted attention in conjunction with the more group-based work.

Current project

These children are assessed on eight components of early numeracy, which are summarised and described below. The children then receive weekly individual intervention (half an hour a week) in the particular components with which they have been found to have difficulty. The interventions are carried out by the classroom teachers, using techniques proposed by myself.

The teachers are released for the intervention (each teacher for half a day weekly) by the employment of supply teachers for classroom teaching. Each child typically remains in the programme for 30 weeks, though the time is sometimes shorter or longer depending on the teacher's assessments of the child's continuing need for intervention. New children join the project periodically.

Components that are the focus of the project

The components addressed here are not to be regarded as an all-inclusive list of components of arithmetic, either from a mathematical or educational point of view. Rather, a few components have been selected because discussion with teachers has indicated their importance in early arithmetical development, and because research (for example, by Dowker, 1998) has shown considerable individual variation in children's performance on these components in the early years.

The components that are the focus of the project include:

- principles and procedures related to basic counting
- use of written arithmetical symbolism
- use of place value in arithmetic
- understanding and solution of word problems
- translation between concrete, verbal and numerical formats
- use of derived fact strategies for calculation
- arithmetical estimation
- memory for number facts.

Remediation for these components principally involves techniques devised by the author, supplemented by exercises and games taken from published materials (for example, Baker and Petty, 1998; Burgess, 1995a; b; Hopkins, 1997a; b; Long, 1996; Straker, 1996). Techniques devised and used by the teachers themselves also play a major role in the project.

The components, and the main intervention techniques, will now be summarised.

1. Principles and procedures related to counting

This component includes: accurate counting of sets of objects; rote verbal counting; understanding of some of the principles involved in counting (as put forward by Greeno, Riley and Gelman, 1984); and repeated addition and subtraction by one. Very basic counting rarely presents problems for six-year-olds, even those who are weak at arithmetic. The areas that are most likely to present difficulties for children in this age group, and which are assessed in the study, are:

a. Understanding of the order irrelevance principle. In other words, the child needs to be able to understand that the result of counting a set of items will not change if the items are counted in a different order, whereas adding or subtracting an item will change the number.
b. Repeated addition by one, where children count a set of items (eight counters in this study) and are asked how many there will be if one more counter is added. This is repeated up to 20.
c. Repeated subtraction by one, where children count a set of items (ten counters in this study) and are asked how many there will be if one is taken away. This is repeated down to zero.

Intervention
For the order irrelevance principle, children practise counting and answering cardinality and order irrelevance questions about very small numbers of counters (up to four), and are then given further practice with increasingly large sets.

For repeated addition by one and repeated subtraction by one, children are given practice in observing and predicting the results of such repeated additions and subtractions with counters (up to 20). They are then given verbal 'number after' and 'number before' problems: 'What is the number before eight?', 'What is the number after 14?', etc.

2. Written symbolism for numbers

There is much evidence, for example from Ginsburg (1977) and Fuson (1992), that children often experience difficulties with written arithmetical symbolism of all sorts, and in particular with representing quantities as numerals (Ginsburg, 1977; Fuson, 1992). With regard to this component, children are asked to read aloud a set of single-digit and two-digit numbers. A similar set of numbers is dictated to them for writing.

Intervention

Children practise reading and writing numbers. Children with difficulties in reading or writing two-digit numbers (tens and units) are given practice in sorting objects into groups of ten, and recording them as '20', '30', etc. They will then be given such sorting and recording tasks where there are extra units as well as the groups of ten.

3. Understanding the role of place value in number operations and arithmetic

This involves the ability to add tens to units (20 + 3 = 23); the ability to add tens to tens (20 + 30 = 50); and the ability to combine the two into one operation (20 + 33 = 53). A related task involves pointing to the larger number in pairs of two-digit numbers, that vary either just with regard to the units (e.g. 23 versus 26); just with regard to the tens (e.g. 41 versus 51); or where both tens and units vary in conflicting directions (e.g. 27 versus 31; 52 versus 48).

Intervention

Children are shown the addition of tens to units and the addition of tens to tens in several different forms:

- written numerals
- number line or number block
- hands and fingers in pictures
- ten-pence pieces and pennies
- any apparatus (e.g. Multilink or Unifix) with which the child is familiar.

The fact that these give the same answers should be emphasised.

Children whose difficulties are more specific to the use of place value in arithmetic may be given practice with arithmetical patterns such as: '20 + 10; 20 + 11; 20 + 12', etc, being encouraged to use apparatus when necessary.

4. Word problem-solving

This component involves: comprehending addition and subtraction story problems of various semantic types (DeCorte and Verschaffel, 1987); selecting the appropriate operations; and solving the problems.

Intervention

Children are given addition and subtraction word problems, which are discussed with them: 'What are the numbers that we have to work with?', 'What do we have to do with the numbers?', 'Do you think that we have to do an adding sum or a taking-away sum?', 'Do you think that John has more sweets or fewer sweets than he used to have?', etc. They are encouraged to use counters to represent the operations in the word problems, as well as writing the sums numerically.

5. Translation between arithmetical problems presented in concrete, verbal and numerical formats

Translation between concrete, verbal and numerical formats has been suggested by several people to be a crucial area of difficulty in children's arithmetical development. For example, Hughes (1986) reported that many primary schoolchildren demonstrate difficulty in translating between concrete and numerical formats (in either direction), even when they are reasonably proficient at doing sums in either one of these formats, and has suggested that this difficulty in translation may be an important hindrance to children's understanding of arithmetic.

The current project includes tasks of translating in all possible directions between numerical (written sums); concrete (operations with counters); and verbal (word problem) formats for both addition and subtraction.

For example, in translating from verbal to numerical, children are presented with word problems (e.g. 'Katie had five apples; she ate two, so now she has three left'), and are asked to 'write down the sum that goes with the story'.

Intervention
Children are shown the same problems in different forms, and shown that they give the same results. They are also encouraged to represent word problems and concrete problems by numerical sums, and to represent numerical problems and word problems by concrete objects.

6. Derived fact strategies in addition and subtraction

One crucial aspect of arithmetical reasoning is the ability to derive and predict unknown arithmetical facts from known facts, for example by using arithmetical principles such as commutativity, associativity, the addition/subtraction inverse principle, etc.

Children are given the Addition and Subtraction Principles Test developed by Dowker (1995; 1998). In this test, they are given the answer to a problem and then asked to solve another problem that could be solved quickly by the appropriate use of an arithmetical principle (e.g. they may be shown the sum $23 + 44 = 67$ and then asked to do the sum $23 + 45$, or $44 + 23$).

Problems preceded by answers to numerically unrelated problems are given as controls. The children are asked whether 'the top sum' helps them to do 'the bottom sum', and why. The actual addition and subtraction problems involved will vary in difficulty, ranging from those which the child can readily calculate mentally, through those just beyond the child's calculation capacity, to those very much too difficult for the child to solve. The particular derived fact strategies that are the main focus of this project are those involving commutativity (e.g. if $8 + 6 = 14$, then $6 + 8 = 14$); the associativity-based N + 1 principle (if $9 + 4 = 14$, then $9 + 5 = 14 + 1 = 15$) and the N − 1 principle (e.g. if $9 + 4 = 13$, then $9 + 3 = 13 - 1 = 12$).

Intervention
Children are presented with pairs of arithmetic problems. The 'derived fact strategy' techniques are pointed out and explained to them; and they are invited to solve similar problems. If they fail to do so, the strategies are demonstrated to them for single-digit

addition and subtraction problems, with the help of manipulable objects and of a number line; and will again be invited to carry out other derived fact strategy problems.

7. Arithmetical estimation

The ability to estimate an approximate answer to an arithmetic problem and to evaluate the reasonableness of an arithmetical estimate is an important aspect of arithmetical understanding. In assessing and remediating this component, children are given a task devised by the author (Dowker, 1997). They are presented with a series of problems of varying degrees of difficulty, and with estimates made for these problems by imaginary characters ('Tom' and 'Mary'). The children are asked: a) to evaluate Tom and Mary's estimates on a five-point scale from 'very good' to 'very silly'; and b) to suggest 'good guesses' for these problems themselves. Once again, the actual addition and subtraction problems involved vary in difficulty, ranging where possible from those which the child can readily calculate mentally, through those just beyond the child's calculation capacity, to those very much too difficult for the child to solve.

Intervention
Children are shown other arithmetical estimates by Tom and Mary and asked to evaluate them. They are encouraged to give reasons for their evaluations.

8. Number fact retrieval

Although most psychologists, educators and mathematicians agree that memorisation of facts is not the essence of arithmetic, Merttens (1996) and others point out that knowledge of number facts does contribute to efficiency in calculation; and Russell and Ginsburg (1984) found it to be a significant factor in distinguishing between mathematically normal and mathematically 'disabled' children. In this study, this skill is principally assessed through Russell and Ginsburg's (1984) Number Facts Test.

Intervention
Children are presented with some of the basic addition and subtraction facts (e.g. $3 + 3 = 6$; $6 + 6 = 12$). They are presented with the same sums repeatedly in the same session and in successive sessions. They also play 'number games' (e.g. some from Straker, 1996) that reinforce number fact knowledge.

Evaluation of effectiveness: some preliminary results

The children in the project, together with some of their classmates and children from other schools, are given three standardised arithmetic tests: the British Abilities Scales Basic Number Skills subtest (1995 revision), the WOND Numerical Operations test, and the WISC Arithmetic subtest. The first two place greatest emphasis on computation abilities and the latter on arithmetical reasoning. The children are retested at intervals of approximately six months.

The project and its evaluation are still in progress. However, the initial six-month and one-year standardised test scores of the first 122 children to take part in the project have been analysed. Not all of the data from 'control' children are yet available, but the first 71 'control' children to be retested showed no significant improvement in standard (i.e. age-corrected) scores on any of the tests. In any case, the tests are standardised, so it is possible to estimate the extent to which children are or are not improving relative to others of their age in the general population.

Results so far have been very promising for the children in the intervention group. The median standard scores on the BAS Basic Number Skills subtest were 96 initially and 100 after approximately six months. The median standard scores on the WOND Numerical Operations test were 88.5 initially and 91 after six months. The median standard scores on the WISC Arithmetic subtest were 6 initially, and 8 after six months. Wilcoxon tests showed that all these improvements were significant. 98 of the 122 children have been retested over periods of at least a year, and have been maintaining their improvement.

A long-term goal is to compare the effects of this project with those of other intervention techniques, and of individual attention as such, so as to assess its specific effectiveness.

Teachers' comments

The reactions of the teachers in the schools concerned have been very positive. They have expressed enthusiasm over the chance to work with children on an individual basis, and feel that the children are enjoying the project and are making considerable improvements. Some of them have said that involvement in the project is also giving them good ideas for general classroom arithmetic teaching.

A few of their comments may serve as an appropriate tentative conclusion at this stage:

> The children are responding very well to the materials and to the extra support . . . They are working through activities linked to basic number skills to establish and reinforce early concepts. Feedback from staff, children and parents has been very positive.

> [The project] has given us valuable information about pupils' learning needs in a core subject, and has provided us with the funding to support the most needy children with individual tuition . . . As a consequence, we have seen the targeted pupils improve considerably in competence and confidence.

> Working with children individually gives greater opportunity for analysing their thinking through individual questioning . . . There is more time and opportunity for using apparatus and asking children to demonstrate what they are doing. These children are often very reluctant to verbalise what they are thinking, and in a whole class or even small group situation, there is not the time to wait for or expect their replies. By giving the children 'thinking time', their confidence and willingness to 'have a go' develops as they offer explanations . . . The children seem to enjoy coming to the sessions and it has been possible to raise their self-esteem in *mathematics in most cases.*

Several teachers considered that this individualised work complemented the classroom-based numeracy work well, to provide a particularly effective combination.

General implications for transformation of learning

There are several implications for effective transformation of arithmetical (and possibly other) learning more generally:

1. The study strongly supports the view that children's arithmetical difficulties are highly susceptible to intervention. It is not the case that a large number of children are simply 'bad at maths'. It is particularly notable that some of the greatest improvement occurred in the WISC Arithmetic subtest: a test sometimes regarded as a measure of predominantly 'innate' intelligence.
2. Individualised work with children who are falling behind in arithmetic has a significant impact on their performance. The amount of time given to such individualised work does not, in many cases, need to be very large to be effective: these children received approximately half an hour a week, and showed considerable benefits.
3. Children are rarely uniformly weak at all aspects of arithmetic. It is misleading and potentially damaging to describe a child as globally 'good' or 'bad' at arithmetic. Although future research will be needed to compare the effectiveness of different types of programme, it appears that diagnosis of, and intervention in, the specific areas of children's weaknesses is likely to prove particularly effective.
4. Collaborations between teachers and researchers are desirable in addressing educational problems.

Acknowledgements

I would like to thank the teachers and children at the following Oxford schools for their participation and collaboration: St Aloysius' First School, St Barnabas' First School, St Ebbes' First School, St Francis' First School, St Michael's First School, New Hinksey First School and Wood Farm First School. I am also grateful to the schools which permitted me to test 'control' children. Professor Sue Iversen of the Department of Experimental Psychology, University of Oxford, is collaborating in the administration of the project. Professors Kathy Sylva and the late John Backhouse of the Department of Educational Studies, University of Oxford, have acted as voluntary consultants. Eve Morris tested some of the 'control' children not participating in the project. The Esmée Fairbairn Charitable Trust is providing financial support for the project. The ESRC funded the research that led up to it.

Some of the material was presented in the conference paper, Dowker, A., Hannington, J. and Tomkys, S. (2000) *Numeracy Recovery: An intervention programme for children with arithmetical difficulties*, presented at ESRC Teaching and Learning Research Programme Annual Conference, Leicester, 9 November.

References

ALBSU (1992) *Literacy, Numeracy and Adults: Evidence from the National Child Development Study*. London: Adult Literacy and Basic Skills Unit.
BAKER, A. and PETTY, K. (1998) *Little Rabbit's First Number Book*. New York: Kingfisher.
BAROODY, A., GINSBURG, H. and WAXMAN, B. (1983) Children's use of mathematical structure. *Journal for Research in Mathematics Education*, 14, 156–68.
BASIC SKILLS AGENCY (1997) *International Numeracy Survey*. London: Basic Skills Agency.

BURGESS, L. (1995a) *Counting: Key Skills in Maths for Ages 5 to 7*. Oxford: Heinemann.

BURGESS, L. (1995b) *Pattern: Key Skills in Maths for Ages 5 to 7*. Oxford: Heinemann.

BUTTERWORTH, B. (1999) *The Mathematical Brain*. London: Macmillan.

CLAY, M. (1985) *The Early Detection of Reading Difficulties: A diagnostic survey with recovery procedures, 3rd Edition*. Auckland, NZ: Heinemann.

DECORTE, E. and VERSCHAFFEL, L. (1987) The effect of semantic structure on first-graders' strategies for solving addition and subtraction word problems. *Journal for Research in Mathematics Education*, 18, 363–81.

DEHAENE, S. (1997) *The Number Sense*. London: Macmillan.

DENVIR, B. and BROWN, M. (1986) Understanding of concepts in low attaining 7–9 year olds. Part 1: Description of descriptive framework and diagnostic instrument. *Educational Studies in Mathematics*, 17, 15–36.

DOWKER, A. (1995) Children with specific calculation difficulties. *Links*, 2(2), 7–11.

DOWKER, A. (1997) Young children's addition estimates. *Mathematical Cognition*, 3, 141–54.

DOWKER, A. (1998) Individual differences in arithmetical development. In C. Donlan (ed.), *The Development of Mathematical Skills*. London: Taylor and Francis.

FUSON, K. (1992) Research on learning and teaching addition and subtraction of whole numbers. In G. Leinhardt, R. Putnam and R. Hattrop (eds), *Analysis of Arithmetic for Mathematics Teaching*. Hillsdale, NJ: Erlbaum.

GINSBURG, H. (1977) *Children's Arithmetic: How they learn it and how you teach it*. New York: Teachers' College Press.

GINSBURG, H., BALFANZ, R. and GREENES, C. (1999) Challenging mathematics for young children. In A. Costa (ed.), *Teaching for Intelligence, II: A collection of articles*. Arlington Heights, Il: Skylight.

GREENO, T., RILEY, M. and GELMAN, R. (1984) Young children's counting and understanding of principles. *Cognitive Psychology*, 16, 94–143.

GRIFFIN, S., CASE, R. and SIEGLER, R. (1994) Rightstart: providing the central conceptual prerequisites for first formal learning of arithmetic to students at risk for school failure. In K. McGilly (ed.), *Classroom Learning: Integrating cognitive theory and classroom practice*. Boston: MIT Press.

HOPKINS, L. (1997a) *Platform Maths 1*. Bath: Leopard Learning.

HOPKINS, L. (1997b) *Platform Maths 2*. Bath: Leopard Learning.

HUGHES, M. (1986) *Children and Number*. Oxford: Basil Blackwell.

LONG, L. (1996) *Domino 1, 2, 3: A Counting Book*. London: Franklin Watts.

MERTTENS, R. (1996) Introduction: primary maths in crisis – what is to be done? In R. Merttens (ed.), *Teaching Numeracy: Maths in the primary classroom*. Leamington Spa: Scholastic.

RUSSELL, R. and GINSBURG, H. (1984) Cognitive analysis of children's mathematical difficulties. *Cognition and Instruction*, 1, 217–44.

SOWDER, J. T. (1992) Estimation and related topics. In D. A. Grouws (ed.), *Handbook of Research on Teaching and Learning Mathematics*. New York: Macmillan, 371–89.

STRAKER, A. (1996) *Mental Maths for Ages 5 to 7: Teachers' Book*. Cambridge: Cambridge University Press.

SYLVA, K. and HURRY, J. (1995) *Early Intervention in Children with Reading Difficulties*. London: School Curriculum and Assessment Authority Discussion Papers, No. 2.

WEAVER, J. (1954) Differentiated instruction in arithmetic: an overview and a promising trend. *Education*, 74, 300–5.

WILLIAMS, C. and WHITAKER, R. L. (1937) Diagnosis of arithmetical difficulties. *Elementary School Journal*, 37, 592–600.

WRIGHT, R., MARTLAND, J. and STAFFORD, A. (2000) *Early Numeracy: Assessment for teaching and intervention*. London: Chapman.

CHAPTER 4

What do children see? A study of children's representations of numbers and operations

TONY HARRIES, RUTH BARRINGTON and CATHY HAMILTON

Background

Over the last few years a main theme for discussion within mathematics education – particularly within the primary sector – is pupils' numerical competence. Much of the discussion emanated from the perception that the performance of English pupils was significantly worse than that of similar pupils in other countries (Harris, Keys and Fernandez, 1997; Keys, Harris and Fernandez, 1996; Bierhoff, 1996). However, it should be noted that the more recent PISA 2000 study seemed to indicate that English 15-year-old students were performing relatively well in mathematical literacy overall.

A term that is being used to encompass this discussion is 'Number Sense' (Anghileri, 2000; McIntosh, Reys and Reys, 1992). This was exemplified by McIntosh et al. (1992) as referring to:

> . . . a person's general understanding of number and operations along with the ability and inclination to use this understanding in flexible ways to make mathematical judgements and to develop useful strategies for handling numbers and operations.
>
> (p. 2)

In their framework for considering number sense they suggest that an important aspect for young children is the development of multiple interpretations and representations of numbers. For example, pupils need to be able to work with number lines *and* number squares *and* place value cards and need to see the connections between the different representations. Further, researchers such as Gray and Pitta (1997), Carpenter, Fennema, Peterson, Chiang and Franke (1989), Carpenter, Fennema and Franke (1993), Carpenter, Fennema, Franke, Levi and Empson (1999) and Thompson (1999) have all discussed the importance of representation in developing mathematical competence. The way we represent mathematical concepts strongly affects the way in which we understand and develop concepts. While place value cards are useful in exploring place value, this particular representation is not so useful for undertaking operations with numbers. Thompson (1999) and Menne (2001) link the idea of representation with pupils' mental methods, which is a major theme within the early years of the National Numeracy Strategy. Dienes' blocks will encourage a different approach to that encouraged by a number line.

In an international study of primary mathematics text books (Harries and Sutherland, 1998) it was found that in other countries – in particular Hungary and Singapore – there was a clear attempt to develop appropriate pictorial representations of different ways of approaching the four operations. The ways in which external representations are used appeared to be quite different in each of the texts analysed. The emphasis in France, Singapore and Hungary is on multiple representations of a mathematical idea, with pupils being explicitly shown the links between representations. Thus pupils will be shown how the number line links with the compensation method of undertaking addition and subtraction, whereas Dienes' blocks encourage thinking in columns as in a standard written method. The intention within the texts is to introduce pupils in a systematic way to a web of interrelated representations which are often introduced as a way of scaffolding pupils in the learning of more standard representations. The critical issues arising from this study were:

- the use of different representations in different national contexts
- the varying ways in which the representations can be used to develop and scaffold conceptual understanding
- the ways in which, in some texts, different representations are linked together.

Consideration of these issues led us to work with a group of Key Stage 2 teachers as they worked on developing the numerical capability of pupils whom they considered to be low attaining. With these teachers we worked on the meaning that pupils associate with number and operations with number. In particular, we have been trying to find out about the mental images that pupils have of number and numerical operations. In this chapter we discuss the way in which pupils work with numbers while performing addition and subtraction calculations and explore the way in which these images might be used to create scaffolds on which pupils can build their understanding of number. In pursuing our work we also investigated the images which pupils have of numbers.

The study

The study was undertaken as part of an INSET programme with 15 Key Stage 2 teachers who wished to focus on issues related to special needs in the normal mathematics classroom. In the college-based sessions generic issues were explored and pupil activities planned. These activities were then undertaken with pupils in school. Data were collected from 346 pupils who were categorised as below:

- high attaining pupils: 110
- average attaining pupils: 149
- low attaining pupils: 87

In total we looked at 973 addition questions and 641 subtraction questions. The distribution is shown in Table 1:

	Addition	Subtraction
High attaining pupils	358 questions	193 questions
Average attaining pupils	388 questions	301 questions
Low attaining pupils	227 questions	147 questions

Table 1. Distribution of questions answered by pupils

The aim of the work was:

- to explore the ways in which pupils explained their approach to addition and subtraction calculations
- to explore the images which pupils have of numbers.

We produced the questions for the teachers and they organised the collection of the data in their classes. The pupils were told that the questions did not represent a test but that we were trying to find out more about how they approached addition and subtraction sums. The teachers identified the pupils as high, average or low attaining pupils – based on their knowledge of the pupils' work in mathematics. While the teachers' main interest was in the approaches of low attaining pupils, the work was undertaken with all pupils in the class. This enabled us to compare the way in which different pupils represented their images and approached their calculations. In addition, we were able to explore how the information gathered might inform work with low attaining pupils in mathematics.

There were three activities with which the pupils engaged – one related to images and two to methods of calculation.

Pupils' calculating strategies

In constructing their mathematical knowledge, two aspects of the pupils' work were considered: the objects with which they work and the processes which they perform on those objects. In mathematics we work with a variety of objects: in number work these will be numbers, fractions, percentages and so on; in shape they will typically be points, lines, 2-D shapes; in algebra the objects might be letters or graphs. Each area of mathematical knowledge is developed by performing processes on the objects being considered. Very early on in their mathematical development, for many pupils, there seemed to have been an emphasis on the processes being performed and the techniques required in order to undertake those processes. This emphasis sees the objects as entities on which processes are to be performed and does not give much importance to the fact that the objects can be understood as the result of processes – for example, seeing 29 as 1 less than 30 enables the pupil to work in a different way with 29.

In developing the work with the pupils we identified the different kinds of addition and subtraction calculations with which the pupils came into contact. Thus 2 + 7 is in a different category from 2 + 9 since the first one remains within the decade but the second one crosses over into the next decade. Similarly 23 + 15 is different from 23 + 18. In the first one there are no crossovers into the next decade whereas there are in the second. With subtraction, 23 − 12 was in a different category from 23 − 17 since, while the second might require decomposition, the first would not. The categories that we used are listed in Table 2, where U is units digits and T is tens:

Addition categories	Subtraction categories
U + U no crossovers	U − U
U + U crossovers	TU − U with no exchange
T + U	T − U
T + T no crossovers	TU − U with exchange
T + T crossovers	T − TU
TU + U no crossovers	T − T
TU + U crossovers	TU − T
TU + T no crossovers	TU − TU with no exchange
TU + T crossovers	TU − TU where U is constant
TU + TU no crossovers	TU − TU with exchange
TU + TU crossover from U only	
TU + TU crossover from T only	
TU + TU crossovers from T and U	

Table 2. Addition and subtraction categories

We gave pupils questions representing each of these categories and from this we identified the strategies used by the pupils as they undertook the calculations. These are illustrated in Figures 1 and 2, which compare the way in which pupils in different attainment groups approached their calculations. The strategies used by the pupils are listed on the right hand side of each graph.

The results of the work illustrated in the graph suggest that:

- high attaining pupils use a greater variety of strategies than other groups
- low attaining pupils predominantly use simple counting strategies for their calculations
- the high attaining pupils were able to 'see' the numerical objects with which they worked in a variety of ways and this led to more flexible ways of working.

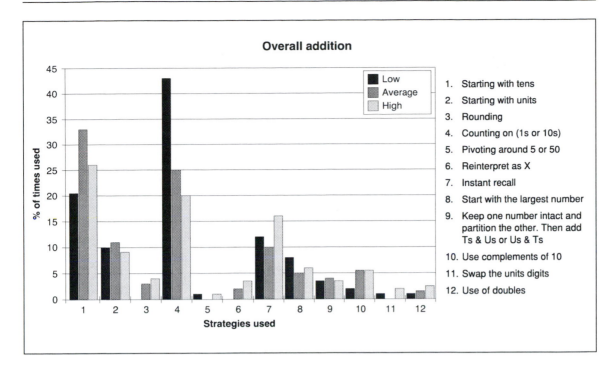

Figure 1. Pupil strategies for addition

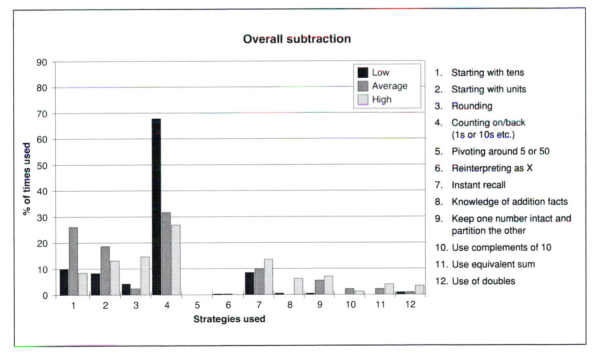

Figure 2. Pupil subtraction strategies

Comments on the results

In analysing the work of the pupils, it would seem that when they were undertaking addition and subtraction calculations there was a clear difference between the way in which the low attaining pupils worked and the way in which the high attaining pupils worked. In working with number calculations the pupils are using numerical objects. Some of these can be considered to be primitive objects – that is, objects for which a consideration of the underlying process by which the object is constructed is not necessary, for example numbers under five. For the low attaining pupils there seemed to be a small number of primitive objects with which they worked. They were also required to work with large numbers, which could be considered to be complex objects for which an understanding of the underlying construction of the number would be useful. When faced with these larger numbers the ways in which the pupils worked differed significantly. The high attaining pupils would use their understanding of the structure of a number to perform the calculation in the most efficient way.

In order to gain an understanding of the way in which the pupils approached the sums, they were asked to write down the strategy they used or, if they were not able to do this, then they would explain to the teacher, who would write down the strategy. In all the examples below the pupils had written the strategies themselves.

4 + 4
I know 5 + 5 is 10 so I took away 2, that gave me the answer. (NS, high attaining, aged 7)

48 + 72
Round up 48 and 72 to 50 and 70. Added together you get 120. Take 2 away because it is 48 and add 2 because it is 72. (AW, high attaining, aged 11)

92 + 69
I took 1 off 92 = 91. Add that 1 to 69 = 70. 70 + 91 = 161. (SB, high attaining, aged 11)

92 + 69
I added 90 + 70 which is 160 but to get from 92 to 90 you take away 2 so I added 2 which is 162 to get from 69 to 70 I added 1 which needed to be took away from 162 which equals 161. (CS, high attaining, aged 11)

77 – 9
I did 77 take away 7 = 70, then 9 – 7 = 2 and then 70 – 2 = 68. (DN, average attaining, aged 9)

80 – 37
I took the 30 from 80 then the 7 = 43. (ST, average attaining, aged 9)

51 – 25
I knew that half of 50 was 25 so I knew the answer was 26. (JS, high attaining, aged 9)

Here we can see that within these two groups there is a range of strategies being used and these pupils seem to be able to use a strategy appropriate to the numbers with which they are working. They would appear to focus on the number and this allows them to use such strategies as working from doubles, rounding, using an equivalent sum, flexible partitioning.

In contrast to this, the low attaining pupils seemed to view the numbers as objects on which specific processes had to be performed. Usually they would apply a simple counting process for completing the calculation. This is illustrated in the examples below (original spellings):

45 + 35
I counted on with my fingers. (SM, low attaining, aged 9)

48 + 23
I counted on top of each other. (SM, low attaining, aged 9)

29 + 5
I first added the 5 and the 9 which was the units. That came to 14. Then I added 2 and 1 which was the tens which made the answer 24. (CN, low attaining, aged 10)

99 + 10
We adit with are fingers. We adit 10 to 99. (AB, low attaining, aged 8)

15 – 5
I work out this by working it out on my fingers. (SF, low attaining, aged 10)

25 – 4
I had 25. I count back 4 and I had the asrer. (SF, low attaining, aged 8)

22 – 17
I did it with bricks. I take 22 and I take 17 from the 22. (TT, low attaining, aged 8)

22 – 17
I started from 22 and then counted down. (JN, low attaining, aged 8)

While it has to be accepted that for some of these pupils the act of writing an explanation of their strategy would cause difficulties, it would seem nonetheless that the only strategy employed by these pupils was one of using basic counting procedures which allow them to use concrete aids such as their fingers or blocks. Thus it would seem that these pupils may have a one-dimensional approach to the calculations, which will inevitably slow down their work as the numbers get more complex. The high attaining pupils appeared to have developed more flexible approaches.

Working with pupil images

Following this work we decided to try to gain some information about the images that pupils developed of numbers. In order to do this the pupils were asked, in their normal lessons, to put on paper any ideas that came into their minds when they thought about numbers. They were told that these were just ideas, that we were only concerned with individual ideas, that differences did not matter and that the work would not be for display. The teachers who undertook this work were asked to get feedback from the pupils on their ideas and to keep a note of any points of interest. When they returned the pupil sheets to us they were asked to indicate each pupil's attainment level. On the basis of the work received from the pupils we identified a number of categories into which the pupil responses appeared to fall. These are listed below:

- *Symbol-based*
  The image here is based on the physical shape of the symbol that represents the number, e.g. simply writing down a few random numbers.

- *Counting-based*
  This is an image related to the idea that counting is a process whereby the number of objects in a set can be represented, e.g. drawing six objects . . .
- *Contextually-based*
  This will tend to be a picture story which gives a context within which number is used, e.g. football players with numbers on their backs.
- *Operation-based*
  This is an image which is based on operational links between different numbers, e.g. $5 = 2 + 3$.
- *Relation-based*
  This is an image which shows a recognition of pattern or order (1 2 3 4 5) or relationships between operations ($2 + 2 + 2 = 3 \times 2$) or within relationships ($2 + 3 = 3 + 2$).
- *Sequence-based*
  This is an image which indicates that the pupils have a sense of sequencing with regard to number, e.g. a number pattern of some kind.

In order to consider the results of this exercise we drew graphs for four age groups and within each age group we compared the number of images demonstrated by pupils of different attainment levels in different year groups ('l' is low attaining; 'a' is average; 'h' is high). These are shown in Figures 3 to 6:

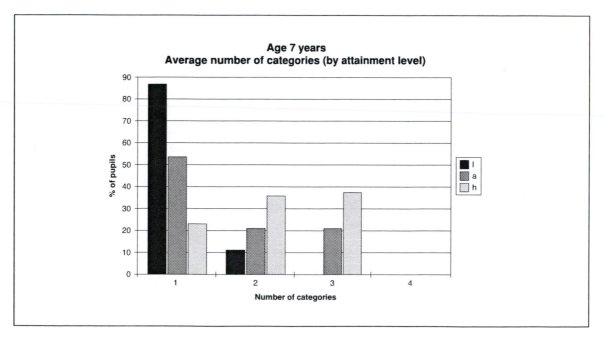

Figure 3. Number images of 7-year-old pupils

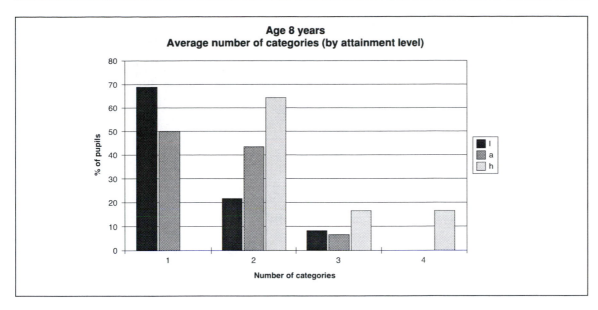

Figure 4. Number images of 8-year-old pupils

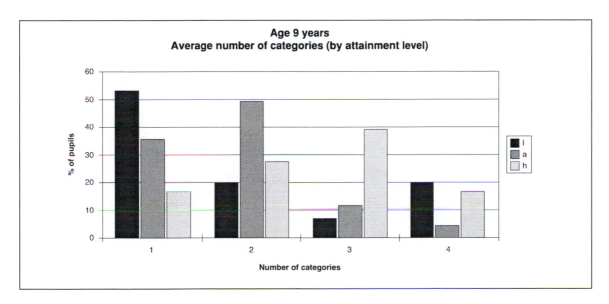

Figure 5. Number images of 9-year-old pupils

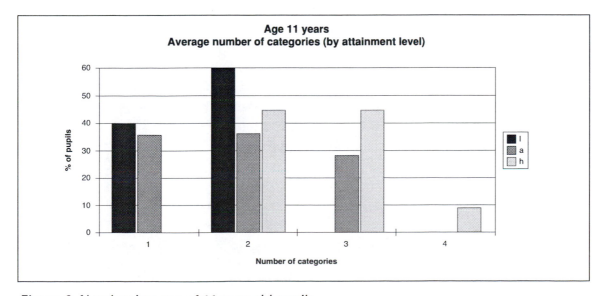

Figure 6. Number images of 11-year-old pupils

As can be seen from the graphs, all the attainment groups show an increase in the number of images they portray as they get older. But it is also clear that high attaining pupils have a wider range of images that they are able to call upon. For low attaining pupils there is still a very large percentage of the pupils who are only able to portray single images of number – even at the age of 11. Further, the results suggest that the dominant image of the low attaining pupils is one of counting and that the counting is generally in ones.

Some implications for teaching

The results of the study suggest a number of implications for teaching. From the work undertaken it would seem that there are particular strategies that low attaining pupils may need to be helped to develop so that they can make choices about the most appropriate way to approach the calculation. These strategies would involve the pupils in focusing initially on the objects/numbers with which they are working rather than the process which they are performing on the objects. In other words, if working with the number 31, they need to see it as 1 more than 30, if working with 28 they need to see it as 2 less than 30 or 3 more than 25 or 8 more than 20. This mirrors some of the ideas in text books from other countries (Harries and Sutherland, 1998). This object focus could lead to a consideration of different strategies. For example, consider $25 + 28$:

- seeing 28 as 3 more than 25 might encourage the strategy of doubling 25 and adding 3
- seeing 28 as 2 less than 30 might encourage the strategy of adding 30 and taking away 2
- seeing 28 as 8 more than 20 might encourage the strategy of adding 20 and then adding 8.

Another important issue concerns the nature of the communication between the pupil and the teacher in developing this range of strategies for calculating. In some instances communication and the understanding derived through this will precede representation. However, on other occasions the representation of these informal strategies may be shared in the classroom and used to aid communication and thus individual understanding. The teacher needs to develop a particular kind of mathematical culture in the classroom which encourages flexible ways of working.

A further didactical consideration is that illustrated in the King's College study on effective teachers of numeracy (Askew, Brown, Rhodes, Wiliam and Johnson, 1997). Here the author identifies characteristics of three orientations of teachers: connectionist, transmission and discovery. Some of the characteristics of the connectionist-orientated teacher are directly relevant to the work discussed above:

- Pupils learn through being challenged and struggling to overcome difficulties.
- Pupils have strategies for calculating but the teacher has the responsibility for helping them refine their methods.
- Numeracy teaching is based on dialogue between teacher and pupils to explore understandings.
- The connections between mathematical ideas need to be acknowledged in teaching.

There is a tendency, particularly with low attaining pupils, for teachers to follow an error analysis route – look for the mistakes – rather than search for the understanding that the pupil is bringing to the task in hand. However, it could be equally important for the teacher to consider the explanations provided by the pupils, since these explanations will reflect the direction in which the pupils are thinking. The role of the teacher will be to explore and broaden the understanding behind the explanations and to help the pupils to adapt their knowledge base. This style of approach to teaching and learning requires teachers and teaching assistants to be confident about developing connections across mathematics and about probing the meaning that pupils give to the numerical tasks that they work on. This approach resonates with the work from the King's College study which found that pupils who worked with 'connectionist teachers' tended to reach higher levels of achievement.

So connectionism seems to be an important way of thinking in developing mathematical competence and confidence – both for teachers and pupils. In the work discussed above it would appear that the pupils who were considered to be of high attainment were the ones who made these connections. Those who were deemed to be low attaining had difficulty with these connections. Thus we need to develop ways in which all pupils have the opportunity to explore connections in all the mathematics that they undertake. The activities/questions below may help teachers and teaching assistants to think about connections and reflect on their practice.

1. How many different ways can you think of for representing numbers?[1]
2. Devise activities for children which require them to represent numbers in different ways.
3. Take a blank page and write any number in the middle of the page. Now fill the page with different ways of thinking about the number – use addition, subtraction . . . Be imaginative!
4. How might you develop this work with children in different year groups?
5. The most important representations for number operations seem to be: beads, the number line, the number square, tens and units blocks. Look back at what you did for number 3. Can you show some of the relationships you used there, in these representations?
6. Try a variety of 2-digit addition and subtraction calculations. Think about different ways in which you might do the calculation. Now think about the way in which you could show these calculations on the representation systems in 5.[2]
7. Think about which representations help us to see connections between addition and subtraction (see Figure 7). Which representations do not help to emphasise this connection?
8. Now think about similar activities for thinking about representations for multiplication and division.

---

1 At Durham University Jennifer Suggate and Tony Harries have been working on the development of a computer program which helps children to explore number representations. Contact Tony at Durham if interested in testing the software: a.v.harries@dur.ac.uk
2 We have also been developing a program which models ways of working mentally using different representations (see Figure 7, p. 50). Contact as in Footnote 1.

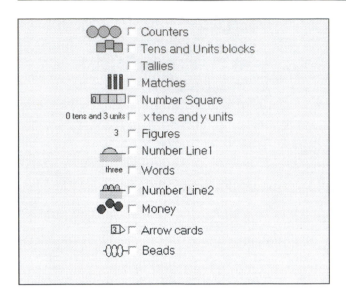

Figure 7. Representations for calculations

References

ANGHILERI, J. (2000) *Teaching Number Sense*. London: Continuum.

ASKEW, M., BROWN, M., RHODES, V., WILIAM, D. and JOHNSON, D. (1997) Effective Teachers of Numeracy: Report of a study carried out for the Teacher Training Agency. London: King's College, University of London.

BIERHOFF, H. (1996) *Laying the Foundation of Numeracy: A comparison of primary mathematics texts in Britain, Germany and Switzerland*. London: National Institute for Economic and Social Research.

CARPENTER, T. P., FENNEMA, E. and FRANKE, M. L. (1993) *Cognitive Guided Instruction: Multiplication and division*. Wisconsin Center for Educational Research: University of Wisconsin-Madison.

CARPENTER, T., FENNEMA, E., FRANKE, M. L., LEVI, L. and EMPSON, S. B. (1999) *Children's Mathematics: Cognitively guided instruction*. Portsmouth, NH: Heinemann.

CARPENTER, T. P., FENNEMA, E., PETERSON, P. L., CHIANG, C. P. and FRANKE, M. L. (1989) Using knowledge of children's mathematical thinking in classroom teaching: an experimental study. *American Education Research Journal*, 26, 449–531.

GRAVEMEIJER, K. P. E. (1994) *Developing Realistic Mathematics Education*. Culemborg: Technipress.

GRAY, E. and PITTA, D. (1997) The nature of the object as an integral component of numerical processes. *Proceedings of the 21st Conference of the International Group for the Psychology of Mathematics Education*.

HARRIES, A. V. and SUTHERLAND, R. (1998) *Primary School Textbooks: An international study*. London: QCA.

HARRIS, S., KEYS, W. and FERNANDES, C. (1997) *Third International Mathematics and Science Study: Second National Report, Part 1*. Slough: NFER.

KEYS, W., HARRIS, S. and FERNANDES, C. (1996) *Third International Mathematics and Science Study: First National Report, Part 1*. Slough: NFER.

McINTOSH, A., REYS, B. J. and REYS, R. E. (1992) A proposed framework for examining basic number sense. *For the Learning of Mathematics*, 12(3), 2–9.

MENNE, J. (2001) Jumping Ahead: An innovative teaching programme. In J. Anghileri (ed.), *Principles and Practice in Arithmetic Teaching*. Buckingham: Open University Press.

PISA 2000. Online at http://www.pisa.oecd.org

SUGGATE, J. (1993) *The Use of Visual Images in Computer Programs for Primary School Mathematics*. Unpublished PhD thesis, Open University, Milton Keynes.

THOMPSON, I. (1999a) Getting your head around mental calculation. In I. Thompson (ed.), *Issues in Teaching Numeracy in Primary Schools*. Buckingham: Open University Press.

CHAPTER 5

Difficulties in extended counting[1]

JENNY HOUSSART

This chapter concerns close observation of a child during normal mathematics lessons. It starts with a consideration of the place of counting in learning mathematics, including possible difficulties. The main part of the chapter is a case study of Julie, a nine-year-old who has difficulties with many aspects of extended counting, in which her response to various mathematical tasks is described in detail. I compiled this case study when assuming a role similar to that of the two learning support assistants who also worked in the classroom. Following the case study, suggestions are made about identifying and helping children who have problems similar to those displayed by Julie. Finally, I reflect on how much I was able to notice in my assumed role and consider the implications of this for LSAs and the teachers they work alongside.

Background

The importance of counting

In recent years there has been growing support for the view that counting has a central role in the development of number concepts (Maclellan, 1997). Work on counting has still tended to have an early years focus, but there has been some recognition of the fact that counting can still be an issue for older children (Thompson, 1997a). Current curriculum guidance, in the form of the *Framework for Teaching Mathematics* (DfEE, 1999a), supports the view that counting can be developed throughout the primary age range. Such developments include being able to count backwards as well as forwards, counting from different starting numbers and counting in different steps. I will refer to these aspects of counting as 'extended counting'. The many references to extended counting in the framework come under the same strand, namely 'numbers and the number system'. The introduction to the framework highlights the importance of this strand by including 'an understanding of the number system' as part of its definition of numeracy. Extended counting is also associated with 'number sense' by Anghileri (2000), who suggests that it helps children develop a feel for number.

1 This article originally appeared in *Support for Learning*, 16(1), 2001, under the title 'Counting difficulties at Key Stage Two' and has been updated for this book

Counting and calculating

Counting also features in guidance about teaching mental calculation strategies (QCA, 1999). This suggests that extended counting is likely to assist children in calculating, particularly using mental methods. One aspect of extended counting is to be able to use starting numbers other than 1. Thompson (1997b) points out that this will help children when adding to move towards a 'count on' rather than 'count all' strategy. For example, they may do 7 + 4 by counting on 4 more from 7. Maclellan (1997) suggests that an ability to count backwards can help children to progress in subtraction, from an initial method based on counting and removing fingers or objects. She asserts that a more sophisticated strategy is to use counting up for the difference aspect of subtraction. Thus children may find the difference between 7 and 3 by counting up from 3 to 7. The Numeracy Strategy includes methods of addition and subtraction based on counting forwards and backwards. Looking through a list of these methods (QCA, 1999, p. 22) shows the progression across the primary age range. It is also worth considering the role of counting strategies in multiplication and division. Anghileri (1997) points out the place that step counting in multiples is likely to have in helping children solve multiplication and division problems. She points out that such counting (e.g. 2, 4, 6 . . .) can be preceded by rhythmic counting, where children say every number but put emphasis on the multiples (e.g. 1, *2*, 3, *4*, 5, *6* . . .). Counting will eventually be replaced by more efficient methods. It is important to consider how children are encouraged to adopt increasingly efficient procedures. Gray (1991) found that many low attaining seven- to twelve-year-olds relied mainly on counting strategies based on objects, fingers or similar means, rather than using a wide range of strategies. More recent work has suggested that it is possible to encourage children to develop more efficient calculating strategies (Askew, Bibby and Brown, 1997). The project described here was carried out with low attaining seven- and eight-year-olds, and was based on an intervention strategy which included extended counting activities.

Counting difficulties

Much of the literature on counting deals with younger children learning to count and confirms that many children get stuck on numbers ending in 9 (e.g. Fuson, 1991; Maclellan, 1997; Thompson, 1997c). Thompson (1997c) also asserts that children in the early stages of counting do not realise it is possible to count using a starting number other than 1. However, for many children these difficulties do not persist and, as Maclellan (1997) remarks, 'counting develops . . . through a process in which the child takes the initiative' (p. 38). Although this may be the case for the majority of children, there are exceptions. Responses to questions on National Curriculum tests reveal that seven-year-old children may still have problems counting across the hundreds boundaries (SCAA, 1997a). The view that some older children may still need help in developing counting skills is supported by the work of Alam, Curtis, Garner, Macadams, Pike and Roberts (1994). In suggesting strategies for helping seven-, eight- and nine-year-olds experiencing difficulties with number, they identify number sequences and patterns as the first of three areas where children may have problems. They put forward a checklist for assessment purposes, which includes extended counting skills such as counting backwards and counting in steps. They also suggest that some children may have developed an ability to carry out calculations on paper, which disguises their limited knowledge. A similar point is made by SCAA (1997b), who suggest that the dominance of formal column calculation in some schools has made it possible for pupils to focus on the single digits within numbers rather than seeing the numbers in a holistic way. Thus pupils' difficulties with the number system may not be exposed.

Summary

The literature suggests that counting is an important skill that is likely to impact on children's understanding of number and enhance their ability to calculate. There is also evidence that extended counting may present difficulties for some children and that these are not always evident, for example in written calculations. The purpose of the case study that follows is to present examples of situations in which difficulties with extended counting are likely to be exposed.

Case study: the story of Julie

Context

The accounts that follow concern Julie, who was nine years old. Her school had three classes in each year group and operated a policy of setting, where children with similar levels of attainment were taught together. Julie was considered to be a 'low attainer' in mathematics and was therefore in the third set. Data were collected using a participant observation approach (Becker and Greer, 1960) in which I assumed a role similar to that of the two learning support assistants who worked on other tables in the classroom. I sat next to Julie and was able to observe and assist her and the other children on the table as they worked on tasks set by the teacher. The incidents related below all concern tasks in which aspects of extended counting could be used. The incidents are taken from my first term in the classroom and are presented in the order in which they occurred.

Subtraction

Julie was working through a worksheet containing vertical subtraction of three-digit numbers, using the method she had been taught, which was to work in columns starting from the units. She worked rather slowly and digits in her answers were sometimes one more or less than the correct answers. When it came to subtracting digits, she took some time and seemed to be using a method similar to finger counting to work out calculations such as $7 - 4$. When Julie came to 'easier' subtractions such as $7 - 1$, she appeared to be using the same laborious method and to be taking just as long. I talked to her about taking one away from numbers and our discussion confirmed she did not have an easy way of doing this. I talked about 'counting backwards', which she initially seemed uncertain about, but she soon joined in when I started a 'countdown'.

Counting coins

It was the first lesson of a block on the topic 'money'. Most of the time was spent working out the total value of piles of coins. Julie found this lesson difficult and at various points I suggested strategies which I hoped might help her. For example, to assist in counting a pile of 10p coins, I suggested counting in tens. She was initially unsure, but joined in when I started. It was a different matter however when we already had 70p made up of a 50p and a 20p and we wanted to count up in tens in order to add on some 10p coins. Julie could not count in tens starting from 70, but needed to start again at 10. Later, when Julie was counting a pile of 2p coins, she counted in ones, touching each coin twice and saying two numbers.

Calculating change

I was paired with Julie in an activity which involved giving change from a pound coin. One person had to specify a price under a pound. The other had to give change from a pound for that price, using a pile of coins. Julie did not seem to have a method for doing this, and provision of coins to count up to a pound was only of limited help as she had such difficulty in counting mixed denominations of coins. We soon moved towards amounts closer to a pound, such as 88p, with Julie using 1p coins to make the amounts up to a pound. This revealed the problem that Julie had in counting across the tens boundaries. For example, she counted to 89 and said she didn't know which number came next. I encouraged her to try and she suggested first 70 then 80.

Using a hundred square

Each child had a hundred square for the first part of a lesson. They were asked to colour in various numbers according to the teacher's instructions. In common with others on the table, Julie often said her answer before colouring in. Her initial spoken answers were sometimes incorrect. However, the result of most of the table saying their answers out loud was that answers were generally agreed on before any colouring in took place. Thus Julie ultimately coloured the correct number in every case. At one point the children were asked to count back 6 from 36 and colour the next number. There was a general consensus that the answer was 30. Julie arrived at the agreed answer despite using the hundred square incorrectly. She moved across the square in the wrong direction dotting each number (including the starting number) with her pencil and counting out loud '1, 2, 3, 4, 5, 6' (see Figure 1).

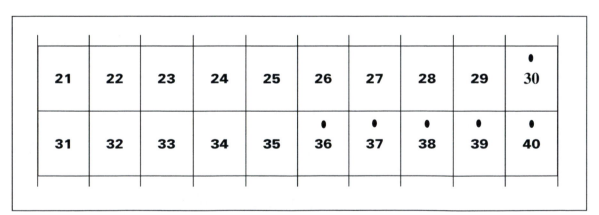

| 21 | 22 | 23 | 24 | 25 | 26 | 27 | 28 | 29 | 30 |
| 31 | 32 | 33 | 34 | 35 | 36 | 37 | 38 | 39 | 40 |

Figure 1. Julie counts back from 36 on a hundred square

Measuring string

During a lesson on measuring, Julie had to measure a piece of string which was longer than her 30cm ruler. I tried to encourage her to suggest a way of measuring it, but without success. We established together that part of it was 30cm long and we marked where that piece ended and placed the mark against the zero of the ruler. The rest of the string was 7cm long, but knowing this did not seem to help Julie. I pointed out that the mark was at 30cm and suggested we count on from there. I started counting at 31 and moving along 1cm as I said each number. Julie slowly joined in and we arrived at an answer of 37.

Measuring the playground
The children were working in the playground estimating various distances, then measuring them using strides. Julie did not ask for help with this activity, and instead of working directly with her, I walked along with the group, striding and counting myself. I was not far behind Julie who counted out loud as she walked, so I was often able to hear her counting. I noticed counting problems at various 'boundaries'. For example, 39 was followed by 90, and 209 was followed by 300. This miscounting was not evident in the answers given when we gathered together afterwards and Julie gave answers very similar to those already offered by other children.

Julie's mathematical profile

The above accounts show that Julie has problems with some aspects of extended counting, particularly counting across boundaries as illustrated by the change activity and the playground measuring. There were other occasions where she did not use aspects of extended counting to help her, for example counting in tens and counting backwards, although she was able to count in these ways.

This is not the whole story of Julie's progress in mathematics. Although she had other difficulties, there were also areas in which she was relatively strong. Compared to other children in the set, she was relatively successful at using standard pencil and paper procedures. She also had none of the physical difficulties with pencil or ruler experienced by some of the children. It was good to see Julie do well in some aspects of mathematics, but I also wondered whether these strengths partly masked the genuine difficulties she had with counting and understanding the number system.

Teaching suggestions

Some extended counting activities are likely to be appropriate for all children in the upper primary years, though for some they may form a relatively small part of their work. If such activities are provided, they are likely to offer reinforcement for most children and highlight those who need further help. Children such as Julie, with particular problems, are likely to benefit from extra activities designed to help them.

Extended counting activities

The oral and mental starter is an ideal place to include counting forwards or backwards, in different steps and from different starting numbers. As well as straightforward counting, it is useful for teachers to be aware of those mathematical activities which are likely to call on an ability to use extended counting. Some of these activities are highlighted in Julie's story, but there are others. Counting in fives, for example, is a skill often assumed when telling the time using analogue clocks. Children reading scales or the calibrations on measuring cylinders may have to count in multiples of, for example, 10 or 100. Using standard masses on balance scales requires the ability to work out the total mass, which may lead to difficulties similar to those which Julie experienced when finding the total of a pile of mixed coins. Children whose difficulties are identified by such activities may need explicit help and additional activities. For example, Julie might need to start by counting piles of coins of one denomination, so she can develop the skills of counting in twos, fives or tens. She could then move on to adding coins to a collection, for example putting 10p pieces in a money box having been told it already contains 40p and counting on from there. Children working with measuring cylinders may need extra practice in reading the calibrations and it may help to relate this to a number line marked in tens or hundreds.

Models of the number system

Models of the number system such as number lines and hundred squares are now widely used in primary schools. However, Julie's experience with the hundred square emphasises the fact that it is not enough just to provide such aids. All children are likely to benefit from reminders about how to use a hundred square or a number line and large versions can be used with the whole class in the oral session at the start of a lesson. Children such as Julie may, however, need additional activities. These may include putting together hundred squares, perhaps in the form of a jigsaw or filling in missing numbers in a section of such a square (DfEE, 1999a). Unfinished squares can also be of different sizes, for example a five by five grid containing the numbers 1 to 25, and can use numbers from different cultures (Alam et al., 1994). Hundred squares can also be used as a board for simple number games, hence reinforcing the direction to go in when counting on. Julie's difficulties with the hundred square also illustrate the fact that initially a number line may be a more helpful model. Number lines of different sizes can be used and Julie may benefit from putting in missing numbers, perhaps around tens or hundreds boundaries, or by putting all the numbers in a given section to reinforce counting from different starting points (DfEE, 1999a; Askew, Briscoe, Ebbutt, Maple and Mosley, 1996). Cut-up sections of a number line can also be put together in the form of a jigsaw (Alam et al., 1994).

Using extended counting skills

For children like Julie, extending their counting skills is only the first step; it is of limited value unless the skills are put to use when required. It may help to make connections between counting and calculating explicit. One possibility here is to relate the oral and mental starter of a lesson to the main teaching activity. For example, counting in fives and revision of the five times table may be an appropriate starter for a session on using analogue clocks. Counting round the class using three-digit numbers may be useful before children embark on measuring activities requiring the use of large numbers. A further strategy is to teach methods explicitly or to reinforce methods suggested by the children. Children can be challenged to explain their 'quick ways' of, for example, subtracting one or adding ten, and these may need additional reinforcement for children who do not easily develop a range of methods themselves. Some children may be aware of an apparently more efficient method, but reluctant to abandon a method which they know works and may need to be encouraged or challenged to use the new method.

The role of the LSA

My role in working with Julie

Some issues arise from the role I assumed during this research. It is important to remember I was not a 'real' LSA. I did not possess the close knowledge of the children I was working with which many assistants have. On the other hand, my knowledge of issues in primary mathematics was of use to me. This raises the question of what LSAs need to know in order to best support children in mathematics lessons and how they can be helped to gain such knowledge and understanding. The other thing that struck me about my assumed role was just how much detail I could observe. For example, I was able to see the way Julie incorrectly moved her finger along the number square and hear her counting out loud when striding across the playground. Given the opportunities LSAs have to see such details, it seems important that such information is shared and used.

Background

Recent research suggests a wide variation in the role of LSAs in different schools (Farrell, Balshaw and Polat, 1999). When the Numeracy Strategy was introduced in 1999, it seemed to carry mixed messages about the role of LSAs and their involvement in training. The *Framework for Teaching Mathematics* (DfEE, 1999a) makes some clear statements about classroom assistants; for instance it states that they should have copies of the framework as well as being aware of the contents of the accompanying vocabulary book (DfEE, 1999b). The framework also talks about assistants being thoroughly briefed about each lesson and says that they should be included in whole-school training days. However, the training materials themselves give a more neutral message about attendance at training days (e.g. DfEE, 1999c).

On the subject of feeding back observations of pupils, Farrell et al. (1999) acknowledge that LSAs are often in a unique position to offer insights into pupil responses. They suggest that immediate verbal feedback is the most effective way of communicating this information, but they also discuss written methods such as the keeping of notes or diaries. In defining effective practice they say it is essential that LSAs contribute to the evaluation of outcomes of lessons. Aplin (1998), in discussing the role of assistants in supporting numeracy, acknowledges the difficulties of adult communication in a busy classroom and offers a written feedback sheet.

Suggestions

My experience of working with Julie leads me to make both general and specific suggestions about the role of LSAs in the Numeracy Strategy. The first general suggestion is that they should have some training for the mathematical aspect of their role. The second is that there should be opportunities to feed back information to teachers about what LSAs have noticed. In some schools both of these things are already established but, as outlined in the section above, there is wide variation. These questions of course lead to wider issues about the pay, conditions and management of LSAs. For example, issues of ability to attend training are raised, as is the question of how the maths coordinator and SENCO might work with LSAs and with each other.

More specifically, I would like to suggest three possible ways in which LSAs might help to identify and assist children with difficulties like Julie's. The first of these is listening to and watching children in order to identify difficulties; the second is use of counting aids; the third is encouraging children to make use of calculating strategies. In the following paragraphs these suggestions are related to extended counting, but all three apply to other aspects of mathematics. They can also be seen as three possible areas in which LSAs could be offered training or support.

Support staff can provide discreet help to children in need of special help in whole-class counting sessions. They may well also have an assessment role in listening to individuals. The assistant might be watching to see if children get lost when the counting switches to using a starting number other than one, or to counting backwards. It is also worth listening especially carefully to see if anyone has difficulties as tens and hundreds boundaries are approached. Assistants may also learn about children's extended counting when working with groups and individuals. When children are counting piles of money, for instance, assistants may be looking to see whether children can count in twos, or whether, like Julie, they touch each coin twice, saying every number. Similarly they can look for the ability to count in fives or tens, including from different starting points, as well as seeing whether children do this spontaneously or need prompting.

Children who need additional activities to help them use number lines and squares are likely to benefit from the help of an LSA. As well as explicitly demonstrating how to count on or back in ones and other numbers, this may include asking questions to help children notice the number patterns present. Children might also be asked about the numbers before or after a certain number, or the number one, or ten more, or less. As well as using number lines for counting, there is the more complex issue of how they can be used for various calculations. Some schools make use of staff meetings or workshops to consider how they are going to use these and other new resources for teaching mathematics. This seems an ideal opportunity to include support staff.

Another possible role for LSAs is in helping decide when children should be encouraged to use a more sophisticated strategy and in providing that encouragement. For example, Julie was able to count in tens but only used this strategy for counting coins when encouraged to do so. Similarly, she needed encouragement to use her ability to count backwards to help her to subtract one from a number. Assistants are often in the position of knowing an individual child well, and know when encouragement to move forward is likely to be appropriate and when it is best avoided. They are also often 'on the spot' at the crucial moment when a child decides how to do a particular calculation.

Conclusion

Although many children extend their counting skills without any direct teaching, we cannot assume that all older primary children have done this. The extension of counting skills is important both in developing children's feel for number and in offering them early calculation strategies. The increase of oral and mental work brought about by the Numeracy Strategy, accompanied by the emphasis on direct teaching, should provide opportunities for the identification and assistance of such children. In many cases this may be a joint task for teachers and LSAs who will need access to specialist knowledge of specific aspects of counting.

References

ALAM, S., CURTIS, B., GARNER, S., MACADAMS, C., PIKE, G., ROBERTS, W. and MAPLE, L. (1994) *A Feel for Number: Activities for number recovery programmes.* London: BEAM.

ANGHILERI, J. (1997) Uses of Counting in Multiplication and Division. In I. Thompson (ed.), *Teaching and Learning Early Number.* Buckingham: Open University Press.

ANGHILERI, J. (2000) *Teaching Number Sense.* London: Continuum.

APLIN, R. (1998) *Assisting Numeracy: A handbook for classroom assistants.* London: BEAM.

ASKEW, M., BRISCOE, R., EBBUTT, S., MAPLE, L. and MOSLEY, F. (1996) *Number at Key Stage 2.* London: BEAM.

ASKEW, M., BIBBY, T. and BROWN, M. (1997) *Raising Attainment in Primary Numeracy.* London: King's College.

BECKER, H. S. and GREER, B. (1960) Participant observation and the analysis of qualitative field data. In R. N. Adams and J. J. Preiss (eds), *Human Organization Research.* Homewood, Ill.: The Dorsey Press.

DfEE (1999a) *The National Numeracy Strategy, Framework for Teaching Mathematics from Reception to Year 6.* Suffolk: DfEE Publications.

DfEE (1999b) *The National Numeracy Strategy, Mathematical Vocabulary.* Suffolk: DfEE Publications.

DfEE (1999c) *The National Numeracy Strategy, Guide for Your Professional Development: Book 2, Effective Teaching and the Approach to Calculation.* London: DfEE.

FARRELL, P., BALSHAW, M. and POLAT, F. (1999) *The Management, Role and Training of Learning Support Assistants.* Nottingham: DfEE Publications.

FUSON, K. C. (1991) Children's early counting: saying the number–word sequence, counting objects, and understanding cardinality. In K. Durkin and B. Shire (eds), *Language in Mathematical Education, Research and Practice.* Milton Keynes: Open University Press.

GRAY, E. M. (1991) An analysis of diverging approaches to simple arithmetic: preference and its consequences. *Educational Studies in Mathematics,* 22, 551–74.

MACLELLAN, E. (1997) The importance of counting. In I. Thompson (ed.), *Teaching and Learning Early Number.* Buckingham: Open University Press.

QCA (1999) *The National Numeracy Strategy, Teaching Mental Calculation Strategies.* Suffolk: QCA Publications.

SCAA (1997a) *Standards at Key Stage 1, English and Mathematics: Report on the 1996 National Curriculum Assessments for 7-year-olds.* Middlesex: SCAA Publications.

SCAA (1997b) *The Teaching and Assessment of Number at Key Stages 1–3.* Middlesex: SCAA Publications.

THOMPSON, I. (1997a) The place of counting in number development. In I. Thompson (ed.), *Teaching and Learning Early Number.* Buckingham: Open University Press.

THOMPSON, I. (1997b) The role of counting in derived fact strategies. In I. Thompson (ed.), *Teaching and Learning Early Number.* Buckingham: Open University Press.

THOMPSON, I. (1997c) Developing young children's counting skills. In I. Thompson (ed.), *Teaching and Learning Early Number.* Buckingham: Open University Press.

CHAPTER 6

John's access to Pythagoras' theorem: inclusion and entitlement in action

MIKE OLLERTON

Some students in mainstream secondary schools do not have opportunities to learn certain mathematical concepts, typically trigonometry and Pythagoras' theorem. Such academic exclusion is often contrived as a result of organisational structures within schools and of decisions taken, based upon assessment of students' past performance, not to teach certain concepts because assumptions are made that some students are unlikely to understand more complex concepts.

In this chapter I argue that it is both feasible and ethically desirable to direct all students onto conceptual 'pathways' to enable access to the whole of the mathematics curriculum, as defined by the National Curriculum. Inclusion to the curriculum is each student's entitlement, irrespective of race, class, gender or the group they are taught in. I draw upon one Year 10 student's written work to exemplify how progress towards a conceptual understanding of Pythagoras' theorem is within the grasp of nearly all. John, in this chapter, had a statement of special educational need which, at the time, was described as 'moderate learning difficulty'.

Planning for access and differentiated outcomes

The depth to which any student makes sense of concepts is dependent upon a variety of factors, some of which are likely to be outside individual teacher's sphere of influence and immediate responsibility (truancy, social difficulties, etc.). I am interested in exploring what, as a teacher, I *can* have responsibility for, in particular short- and medium-term lesson planning which takes account of students' inevitably different learning. This, in combination with realistic expectations that all students can achieve some level of understanding of more complex concepts, forms the basis of my belief that all students can be provided with opportunities to access the entire statutory school curriculum.

When making medium-term plans for groups of lessons leading to students developing their understanding of any concept, it is important to consider what underpinning knowledge students will need to work from. For Pythagoras' theorem, being able to count or work out an area of shape and knowing what a right-angled triangle looks like are both useful, and students will have engaged with such ideas frequently in the past. There are other desirable, generic qualities for students to develop, such as being confident to 'have a go' and not being afraid of being 'stuck'. Mathematical qualities would include knowing how to explore ideas and problems, searching for pattern and looking for connections . . . and being willing to do so.

Expecting students to explore ideas is a key principle in my teaching. My starting point for the first in a group of lessons about Pythagoras' theorem is to:

- draw some 'slanted' lines on a square grid
- define each line as a vector
- draw a square on each vector
- count the area of each square
- look for a connection between the values that define the vector and the area of the resulting square.

How I set up this sequence of tasks, how didactic I choose to be, whether I use pegs and pegboards and ask students to play a 'game' of *4-in-a-square* (see below), whether I encourage discussion groups or ask students to work in pairs are all professional lesson-planning decisions I must take.

> *4-in-a-square* is a game played by pairs of students. Each has pegs of one colour and they take turns to place their pegs in a square-grid pegboard. When one person has placed four pegs on the vertices of a square of any orientation, the 'game' is finished. These four points are then recorded on square grid paper. One side of the square can be recorded in vector notation and the area of the resulting square calculated.

Because John was taught mathematics in a non-setted group, I was aware that he and others might require specific attention once the class had begun to engage with the tasks described. However, this was no different to needing to give my attention to other stronger mathematicians at different times during the sequence of lessons over the following two or three weeks. What I wanted was for John to be able to make a start. Once he had the confidence to do so I knew, from past experience, that he would develop his work accordingly with determination and endeavour.

Planning a range of extension tasks was fundamental. I would suggest these to different students as they demonstrated their understanding that the area of the square could be calculated by squaring the values for the horizontal and vertical components of the initial vector and adding these together. This is essentially how Pythagoras' theorem works.

Extension tasks were as follows:

a. Calculate the length of the vector once we knew the area of the square so formed.
b. Transform each vector into a right-angled triangle
   Through individual and small group discussion I gave students input on how the vector could be seen as the hypotenuse of a right-angled triangle. I wished students to make the significant connection between the area of the slanted square and the area of the square on the hypotenuse of a right-angled triangle; similarly, that squaring the values of the components of the vector was equivalent to drawing squares on the other two sides of the right-angled triangle.
c. Develop ideas of finding a square root.
d. Draw some life-size, right-angled triangles on a square grid and using what students had learnt to calculate the length of the hypotenuse.
   At various points in lessons I would have a didactic conversation with students and tell them the relevant vocabulary.

e. Draw some life-size, right-angled triangles on plain paper, measure the lengths of the two shorter sides and using this information to calculate the length of the hypotenuse.

Students would work with values that were not whole numbers and check that the calculator answer was the same as the measured length of the hypotenuse (to the nearest millimetre).

f. Write a short program on a graphical calculator that carried out Pythagoras' procedure.

Groups of students were taught how to write simple programs on graphical calculators in Year 7 and developed this skill to write more complicated programs in Years 8 and 9.

g. Calculate one of the shorter sides of a right-angled triangle given the lengths of the other two sides.

h. Solve problems in 3-D, such as calculating the length of the 3-D diagonal in a cuboid.

John's write-up on Pythagoras' theorem

All students were asked to produce a written record of the work they had done and what they had understood. Students either wrote up as they went along or carried out this task at home. Sometimes specific lessons were used for students to write up their work.

I had suggested to John that he might begin by drawing vectors which all had a vertical component of 1, and the first two pages of his write-up contained nine such diagrams showing how he had calculated the area of each. He produced a table of results as follows:

V	A
9 1	82
4 1	17
5 1	26
6 1	37
7 1	50

John added the following commentary (original spelling):

> *Wot this graf* (table) *shows is the arur veturs and the pattern is if you ×2 9* [square 9] *then + 1 = 82 and It dus that all the way tbaw* (down).

My next conversation with John was to suggest he draw some different vectors and squares so that neither component was 1. He proceeded to produce a second set of diagrams and a table of results as follows:

V	A	
$\binom{4}{2}$	20	$4 \times 4 = 16 + 4$
$\binom{5}{2}$	29	$5 \times 5 = 25 + 4$
$\binom{6}{2}$	40	$6 \times 6 = 36 + 4$
$\binom{7}{2}$	53	$7 \times 7 = 49 + 4$
$\binom{8}{2}$	68	$8 \times 8 = 64 + 4$
$\binom{9}{2}$	85	$9 \times 9 = 81 + 4$

John had written a calculation next to each line showing a pattern emerging. There is clearly much repetition here and he was effectively practising and consolidating his knowledge of vectors and calculating areas of squares. A key learning objective was that John was in control of how much information he produced and, therefore, how many examples he needed to do in order to see a pattern emerging. There are important issues here about choice and about students determining for themselves how many calculations they need to do in order to make sense of the mathematics. This is different from the teacher making such decisions on behalf of students. Although the calculations in the third column of the table are not 'mathematically' correct because he has misused the equals sign, I was confident that John knew the connection between the values for each vector and the area of each square. As a consequence of conversations with John I gained a much wider perspective on his achievement and believed he gained a deeper understanding than the result of any test could reveal. John's write-up totalled eight pages and he developed his work as far as the fourth extension task above.

Access and inclusion: teaching SEN-statemented students in a mainstream, non-setted group

The curriculum was structured upon accessible starting points with ranges of planned extension tasks. All students were provided with the same starting points for every module of work. Through such a structure John had opportunities to demonstrate what he could do and, like other students, had opportunities to develop his understanding of mathematical concepts commensurate with his work rate, drive, interest, cognitive aptitude and all other qualities which are often construed as constituting 'ability'.

One outcome of John having a statement of special educational need was for him to be withdrawn from certain lessons and taught in a small group of students in a support unit. In some subjects John was placed in 'bottom' sets; as such he was not in a position to access some areas of the curriculum, irrespective of whether he would have been capable of doing so. John was not withdrawn from mathematics although on some occasions he had in-class teacher support. Teaching John in a non-setted group was a pleasure, this despite or perhaps because of the difficulties he had with mathematics.

He set a tremendous example to his peers, frequently demonstrating positive attitudes to his work. As his teacher I constructed a wider range of strategies to help him learn mathematics; in this way John helped me become more effective for *all* students.

Neither John nor his classmates were unaware that he found mathematics difficult. However, he rarely appeared daunted by his more mathematically capable and competent peers or by the fact that some usually worked on more complex ideas. John just 'got on' with the work he could do and learnt that asking for help was more important than struggling in silence. Because different students required different amounts of input at different times, situations frequently emerged where students who knew the connection took responsibility for explaining what they knew to other students. In this way there were occasions when there was more than one 'teacher' in the room. All these elements – students being encouraged to work at levels commensurate with their current levels of understanding, students deciding when and from whom they might gain help, and students being encouraged to help each other – were part of the atmosphere and the culture of the classroom (Ollerton and Watson, 2001, p. 13).

I could anticipate that John would not necessarily engage with concepts to the same depth or at the same level of complexity as some of his classmates. However, this did not mean having low expectations and therefore deciding in advance not to offer him exactly the same starting points to modules as everyone else. I expected he would work on a common set of mathematical concepts and study them to a depth commensurate with his capability.

One of the key features of the classroom was the absence of a single 'pace' or 'level' at which individuals worked. Nor were there 'top', 'middle' and 'bottom' levels and paces of work rate; there existed as many levels of response to tasks offered as there were students in the class. An important part of the culture of the classroom was that students took responsibility for the complexity to which they developed any task. Students understood that they were the ones who had to do the learning and that I could not do this learning for them. Some students' work was published (Sutcliffe, 1989, p. 26–7; Ashworth with Ollerton, 1995, p. 9).

Over time there grew within the class a respect for John; he both benefited from and was a benefit to others. His presence in the class did not 'slow' other students down, indeed he was a valuable determinant for helping more 'gifted' students realise their own good fortune at being able to make sense of school mathematics without so much struggle. This spurred some to extend their own mathematics beyond the GCSE syllabus.

By learning in a non-setted group, therefore, John was integrated into a mainstream class and worked on the same mathematics curriculum as his peers. By working from the same starting points as everyone else, in mathematics lessons, he was included academically. Such academic inclusion had a positive effect on John's social and emotional development and upon the humility and humanity of his peers.

References

ASHWORTH, K. with OLLERTON, M. (1995) *You Need to Use the Calculator*. Micro Math 11/3. Derby: ATM.
OLLERTON, M. and WATSON, A. (2001) *Inclusive Mathematics 11–18*. London: Continuum.
SUTCLIFFE, D. (1989) *Partitioning Numbers*. Derby: ATM.

CHAPTER 7

Count me out: task refusal in primary mathematics

JENNY HOUSSART

Introduction

This chapter reports research carried out with low attaining pupils in primary mathematics lessons. The question considered is whether there is a relationship between children's apparent refusal to carry out a mathematics task and the task's nature. The question arose as a fusion of my initial research interests and one of the many concerns of the teachers I was working with. My research into tasks in primary mathematics classrooms concerned both the selection and adaptation of tasks by teachers and how children responded to them. The teachers had to consider the potentially challenging behaviour of some of the children; one of their concerns was to try to keep children involved and behaving in an acceptable way. I identified incidents in which children behaved in an unacceptable way which included refusing to do the task set, often accompanied by visible signs of dissent. I was interested in the task the child was supposed to be doing at the time. My aim was to ascertain whether particular types of task triggered refusal.

Background

In focusing on the task children were supposed to be engaged in when they refused to cooperate, I was looking at just one among many potential factors. These include the mood of the child, relationships and factors outside the classroom. My intention was therefore to learn more about one possible contributing factor to children's behaviour. My approach was derived from the advice of Margerison and Rayner (1999) on assessing classroom behaviour. They advocate the use of observation data to gather information stating that, 'The intention is to know: first, what a pupil does; second, how often; and third, in what situations' (p. 90).

The lessons observed all took place in English primary schools following the introduction of the National Numeracy Strategy and therefore broadly followed the approach advocated by the strategy (DfEE, 1999). Although in practice there was variation in how far the strategy was followed, some aspects were seen in most lessons. These included the use of direct teaching and use of an oral or mental starter followed by a main teaching activity. The *Framework for Teaching Mathematics* (DfEE, 1999), the principal document associated with the strategy, also offers brief advice on teaching pupils with special educational needs. It points out that problems with mathematics are often, but not always, accompanied by literacy problems. Pupils with emotional or behavioural difficulties can benefit from the structures and routines advocated, it is claimed. Of such pupils it is said, 'Tasks and timings are critical; you need to consider them carefully if you are to maintain the pupils' motivation and interest' (p. 23).

Much of the existing research on tasks stems from the work of Doyle and his definition of an 'academic task' (Doyle, 1983). He conceptualised tasks as having three elements, namely a goal or product, a set of resources available to students while generating the product and a set of operations which can be applied to the resources to reach the goal. Classifications of tasks include that suggested by Christiansen and Walther (1986), building on Polya (1966) in distinguishing between routine tasks (exercises) and non-routine tasks (problems). Skemp (1979) makes a similar distinction contrasting 'routine' actions and activities with those which are 'novel'. Research demonstrates that level of difficulty is a factor considered by teachers in task selection. Research on tasks in British primary schools enumerates problems involved in matching level of difficulty to the children involved (Bennett, Desforges, Cockburn and Wilkinson, 1984). It is also acknowledged that tasks presented in the form of text books, worksheets or workcards may present pupils with reading and interpretation difficulties (Shuard and Rothery, 1984).

The issue of setting is also relevant to the current study. Setting is acknowledged as a possibility in the *Framework for Teaching Mathematics* (DfEE, 1999), but not particularly advocated. However, setting is seen by schools as advocated by inspectors (OfSTED, 1998) and its use in primary schools has grown in recent years (Sukhnandan and Lee, 1998). Concern about the recent growth in setting is expressed by Ollerton (see Chapter 14), who raises issues such as equality of opportunity, and questions whether setting is compatible with inclusion. A slightly different view is put forward by Aylett (2000), reporting on an evaluation of the introduction of broad band setting in her school. She found that the majority of pupils, including those in the lowest band, expressed a preference for setting. In discussing this finding, she suggests that pupils can have positive experiences whatever the system of grouping, and points to factors such as high expectations of teachers in making the difference. There has also been a call for consideration of how setting affects pupils' understanding of mathematics (Boaler, Wiliam and Brown, 2000), with the need for qualitative research including classroom observation being pointed out. My own previous work suggests that setting does have an effect on the tasks teachers select for children, more challenge being offered to 'higher' sets and more step-by-step approaches being used for 'lower' (Houssart, 2001).

Contexts

This work is drawn from observations carried out in two schools over two years. Both schools operated a policy of setting for mathematics, where children considered to have similar levels of attainment were taught together. All my observations were carried out with lower sets, and the majority of the children were considered to be in the lowest 25% as far as attainment in mathematics was concerned. Two of the sets contained Year 5 children (nine- and ten-year-olds) and one was a mixed set of Year 3/4 children (seven, eight and nine years old). A participant observation approach was used. I adopted a role similar to that of the classroom assistants working in both classrooms. In the Year 5 classroom I sat at the table with groups of children. In the Year 3/4 class I did the same when children were working at tables, but sat round the edge of the group with the other adults when they were working 'on the mat'. My role therefore varied according to the activity. Although it was almost entirely observational when the teachers were engaged in direct teaching, my participation was higher at other times. Hence there was a need to acknowledge that my actions may sometimes have had a bearing on events.

Both teachers were experienced and had clear expectations of behaviour. For most of the time most of the children met these expectations. However, despite the teachers' best efforts, some children occasionally broke the accepted rules of behaviour, for example by opting out of the task.

Identifying incidents

There is a clear difficulty in defining 'opting out'. It is not possible to know whether a child is opting out of listening to an explanation or trying to understand. When children are working individually it is sometimes possible to see who is working and who isn't, but harder to judge whether pauses are for genuine reflection or represent disengagement from the task. It is also unrealistic to expect to identify whether every child in a class is on task at any given time. Therefore my initial focus was on the easiest categories to judge. I looked at whole-class activities and noted those children who seemed to be clearly opting out of the task required, either because they were not doing what they should be, or because they were doing something they shouldn't. Children in the first category, for example, were not joining in when the whole class was counting aloud or not holding up answers using number fans when asked to do so. I was particularly interested in children who failed to join in when reminded or encouraged, rather than those who seemed to have short lapses of concentration and joined back in when prompted by adults. Children in the second category were engaged in diversions such as playing with cards or leaning back on their chairs or sitting with their back to the teacher during whole-class discussion. As I became aware of children apparently prone to opting out, I also looked more closely at whether they were on task at other times, for example during individual written activities.

Even the fairly simple definition of opting out adopted to start with proved problematic for three reasons. The first was that some children apparently sending signals that they were not doing something turned out, on closer inspection, to have actually done it. I will refer to these incidents in my discussion as 'fake opting out'.

Example 1. Lawrence – 'fake opting out'

Lawrence was a large Year 5 boy with an interest in rugby. He was sometimes loud, so his presence in the classroom could be dominant. On one occasion the children were supposed to be completing a worksheet quietly, but Lawrence was out of his seat and whistling, which led to him being kept in at lunchtime. The worksheet in question was about multiplying single digit numbers by two and required the children to put answers in boxes. Lawrence had started filling in answers while the sheets were given out and continued to do so while the teacher was explaining the work. It was only when the children were asked to start work that his disruptive behaviour started, but a glance at his worksheet while he was out of his seat confirmed that the sheet was completed correctly.

There were other incidents of fake opting out in which I was able to see the children's work, either at the time or later. In all these cases the work was mostly or entirely correct, yet the children had apparently given it minimal attention and spent very little time on it. This raises the issue of level of difficulty of the work set, which will be considered later.

The second problem in identifying incidents was that my original intention was to look only at children refusing to do an activity, rather than those genuinely unable to do it. I identified incidents as 'opting out' only if a child signalled refusal to cooperate, by saying something like, 'I'm not doing this, it's stupid.' I did not consider a child to be opting out of a task if they put their hand up and asked for adult help because they could not read the words. However, these could be seen as different ways of dealing with the same problem and some children seemed to prefer refusal to the latter course. I still recorded these incidents, but acknowledged that opting out was sometimes 'tactical'.

Example 2. Jodie – 'tactical opting out'

Because of her history of challenging behaviour, Jodie worked near a classroom assistant most of the time. Despite minor difficulties, she usually participated in the work of the class. However, on one occasion she refused a task involving copying from the board. She made her refusal clear and made rude noises instead. She was kept in to complete the task at lunchtime and was moved to sit in front of the board. When I went to see how she was getting on she had made little progress and asked me about one of the words. I helped by pointing to words and later by spelling them out. In this way the task was eventually completed.

In including the above incident, I need to acknowledge my own involvement. Although my interaction with Jodie may have had an effect on her completion of the task, it also gave me some clues about her possible reasons. As I recorded incidents, it emerged that I was observer only in the majority, but when I was involved in incidents I had more detailed information about them.

A further problem was that there were occasions when it seemed likely that individuals were not going to cooperate whatever the task, as their intentions had been signalled before the task was presented. This usually arose when children arrived at the mathematics lesson upset or angry. I will refer to such incidents as 'predetermined opting out'. I originally questioned the point in noting the tasks involved in incidents of predetermined opting out, as these children seemed likely to opt out whatever the task. However, there was a point. In all cases of predetermined opting out, the child did eventually opt back in at some point in the lesson. In these cases I was particularly interested in the task into which the child had opted back.

Example 3. Penny – 'predetermined opting out'

Penny moved schools during the year and did not settle easily. Her body language during whole-class discussions suggested she was not interested and on one occasion she was reading a magazine while the teacher was explaining work. There were several occasions when the work became more difficult and Penny joined in. Some of these incidents involved calculations – the one described here involved classifying 2-D shapes. Penny had appeared disgruntled in the early part of the lesson when the teacher revised the names of common shapes such as circle, rectangle and triangle. However, later in the lesson, the teacher included concave quadrilaterals in the selection of shapes presented. Penny's hand went up immediately the teacher started asking questions; she was clearly curious about these new shapes which were, as she put it, 'bent in'.

Classifying incidents

Having classified incidents as 'opting out' I sought patterns and explanations. I did this partly by looking for similar incidents when similar tasks were presented. I also sought other information about factors I felt could be problematic, such as reading ability. I then developed a possible categorisation of types of task prompting opting out by certain children.

Tasks provoking opting out may be grouped into three categories, occurring with unequal frequency. The most common incidents related to the level of difficulty. Next was the mode of presentation. The third category concerned calculation tasks, where a particular method was stipulated which did not match the method used by the child.

The most common type of task provoking opting out was one where the level of difficulty was inappropriate for the child. Perhaps surprisingly, the majority of incidents concerned tasks which were too easy. There were three main reasons for suggesting that in the incidents observed the tasks were too easy. The first concerned 'fake opting out' when the task was actually completed very quickly, as in the example given earlier of Lawrence and the worksheet. The second was by comparison with harder tasks on the same topic which children had completed successfully. For example, there was a group of boys who had mixed success with tasks during a block of work on fractions. A detailed look at their response to different tasks suggested that they were more successful on the more challenging tasks. The third was because in incidents of predetermined opting out children sometimes opted back in when a harder task was presented. This suggested that they may have been opting out of tasks which they perceived as too easy for them.

Example 4. Craig – level of difficulty

Craig had originally been in a higher set, but I suspect he was moved because of discipline problems and at times his behaviour was of concern to the school. On this day he had not appeared for maths at the start of the lesson but was later found, brought in by the head of year and asked to sit at the table where I was working with Penny. He sat with his arms folded and his back to the teacher, who was concluding the early part of the lesson with the calculation 'five add nine'. The main task was then explained, though Craig did not seem to listen. Penny made some comments to me about the task and although they were neither to Craig nor about him, he responded each time by saying 'So?' in an aggressive way. My attempts to encourage Craig to start work failed. Meanwhile Penny encountered difficulties with the task. It was presented in the form of a puzzle, but involved addition of two-digit numbers in horizontal format. Penny had done 35 + 19 + 36 and arrived at the answer 720. She stood by her answer, despite my questioning, so she explained her method. She had added the tens getting 7 which she had written down first, then added the units getting 20. We talked about this and I helped her to adapt her method to get the correct answer. By the end of the discussion Craig was openly listening and gave his assent to the final answer. I suggested that he write the answer on his sheet and Penny invited him to come round to our side of the table so we could work together. He did so and we discussed ways of doing the next calculation.

There is a need to consider the effect of my involvement in this incident. In my assumed role I did try to encourage children to participate, as did the other classroom assistants I worked alongside. The crucial point in the incident above is that not all forms of intervention worked. This was the first time I had worked near Craig, hence I had not built up a relationship with him, and my initial attempts to get him to participate failed. My action in discussing an apparent mathematical contradiction with Penny was aimed at assisting her rather than interesting Craig, yet it seemed to achieve both ends.

Some children apparently opted out of tasks presented in certain ways. Many of these incidents fell into the 'tactical opting out' category, with doubt about whether the child had the skills, usually non-mathematical, to do the task. An example was Jodie, as described above. A slightly different example is Claire, a Year 3 girl, who showed a preference for written as opposed to practical or oral tasks.

Example 5. Claire – mode of presentation

One lesson providing a clue to Claire's preferences was an introduction to addition. The children were on the mat, adding the spots on dominoes. A 'double one' domino was produced and Claire was asked how many spots there were altogether. She did not answer despite encouragement from the classroom assistant. This was a longer than usual practical and oral session and prompted Claire to ask, 'Are we doing games all day?'

The following week the children were working on an activity called number walls, adding numbers and recording answers on a sheet. Claire carried out this task correctly and willingly using a number line. She had to be reminded to count 'one' when she had added one on, rather than on the starting number, but had no problem with the idea of starting on the bigger number rather than counting from zero.

Another clue to Claire's task preference can be found by studying one of her 'bad days'. One such day started with Claire refusing to join the circle for a counting game and ended with an adult's decision to put her on an individual behaviour plan. During the lesson Claire declined to participate in some tasks and only participated reluctantly in others, with a great deal of adult support. There was one exception, a task where children came to the board to write numbers. When this task was introduced, Claire signalled her willingness to participate by sitting up straight and folding her arms. She was soon chosen to write an odd number on the board and did this correctly.

A less common category of opting out only applied to some kinds of task. There were occasions when the teachers stipulated that calculations be done in certain ways, often with everyone calculating together and children giving interim answers. This sometimes led to opting out by children whose method of calculation did not match the one used by the teacher.

Example 6. James – method of calculation

James was in Year 4 and had a statement of special educational needs. He had moderate learning difficulties and coordination problems. The first time I noticed James not doing the task required was when the children were being asked to add numbers using the 'count on' method. For example, for 4 + 3 the teacher said, 'Put four in your head and count on three'. The children held up three fingers and used them to count on '. . . five, six, seven'. James was asked to join in, first by the teacher, then by the support assistant who works with him. Later in the same lesson I worked with James on a task involving similar calculations. He got the answers correct, but arrived at them using cubes and the count all method. James was always reluctant to participate when 'count on' was used. In one lesson children were told to put eight in their head and count on four more. The teacher encouraged James to join in and he reluctantly did so, eventually reaching 12. The assistant nearest James then revealed that he had actually reached the answer 12 earlier and told her. In the next calculation the teacher tried to get James to count on four from nine. She gave him a clue by saying, 'James, nine, t . . .' He responded by saying 'twenty'. James seemed either unable or unwilling to use the method to add, but could usually carry out the calculations in a different way.

Extending the model

Although there were several incidents in each category, they occurred relatively rarely and were confined to a relatively small number of children, most of whom had a history of potentially challenging behaviour. Most of the children, most of the time, did not refuse so publicly to do the tasks set. However, closer observation when the categories were being identified suggested that the relatively small number of opting out incidents was supported by a larger number of incidents where children found tasks of a certain type difficult, disliked doing them or silently withdrew from participation. This was true for all three categories.

Many children seemed to have difficulties with tasks presented in certain ways and to have preferences for mode of presentation. Difficulties in reading and writing were part of this, with copying from the board and drawing charts and tables causing problems. Often children complained about these tasks or asked for help. Some children had a preference for written tasks, but a disinclination to be involved in oral work. One child had difficulties with the keyboard, making computer tasks difficult. Another boy, in contrast, performed better on tasks using the computer than on similar tasks presented in other ways.

Many children appeared less motivated when the work got easier, but a few reacted negatively when it got harder. Some children expressed anxiety to me about whether they would be able to do tasks given in the main part of the lesson. There were also some who made no attempt to participate when extension questions were asked or explanations sought.

In sessions where certain styles of calculation were expected there were children encountering difficulties. Some appeared not to move forward and use the mental methods suggested, preferring to use equipment or methods based on counting. Some preferred mental methods with numbers treated holistically, but became lost when standard methods were used dealing with single digits.

The two teachers had different styles and preferences. One emphasised the oral methods advocated by the Numeracy Strategy; the other continued to use standard written methods. One reduced reading and recording to a minimum, the other made frequent use of standard tasks on worksheets or recorded in maths books. In both cases there were children who shared the teacher's preferences and those who did not. It was more a case of what suited individual children than of a 'correct' approach or one in line with the Numeracy Strategy.

Implications

This research raises many issues. We could wonder, for example, about the tendency of some young children to prefer to be seen to refuse a task than to be seen as unable to do it.

The main mathematical issue raised is the way many children preferred more challenging tasks. Sometimes it was just a case of the task getting harder, at other times it was making it less routine or repetitive. Sometimes, as in the story of Penny and the concave shapes, an element of surprise engaged children. At other times, as with Craig and the addition task, it was an apparent contradiction that attracted their interest. This accords with Trickett and Sulke's findings (1988) who, building on the 'Low Attainers in Mathematics Project' (1987), suggest that low attaining students are able to cope with activities involving elements of mathematical challenge, including a temporary state of confusion or puzzlement.

Other issues include the need to present activities in different ways. This is an assessment as well as a teaching issue, as some of the children I observed performed very differently on mathematically similar tasks presented in different ways. The issue of methods of calculation is perhaps harder and here it may be a case of choice rather than variety, with different methods allowed if they suit the children. This does not mean never trying to move children forward to use more economic or efficient methods, but that this is best done with an awareness of what individuals are ready for, and an acceptance that children have different calculating preferences.

Conclusions

My findings are open to different interpretations. The most striking finding was that whenever a child refused to do a mathematical task, there was a possible explanation in the nature of the task, even if other factors contributed. Even those children coming to mathematics lessons apparently unprepared to do anything eventually opted in as different tasks were offered, and there was always a possible explanation in the nature of the task itself.

I therefore believe that when children refuse to do a piece of mathematics, it is vital to analyse exactly what they are refusing to do.

I believe this work has wider implications. The three categories of problems with tasks identified, namely level of difficulty, mode of presentation and method of calculation, were helpful in considering the work of other children, not just the task refusers. Considering these three factors when planning tasks and, especially, offering variety or choice within each category, is likely to benefit all children. Therefore lessons derived from this study of 'special children' may have wider relevance.

References

AYLETT, A. (2000) Setting: Does it have to be a negative experience? *Support for Learning*, 15(1), 41–5.

BENNETT, N., DESFORGES, C., COCKBURN, A. and WILKINSON, B. (1984) *The Quality of Pupil Learning Experiences*. London: Lawrence Erlbaum Associates.

BOALER, J., WILIAM, D. and BROWN, M. (2000) Students' experiences of ability grouping – disaffection, polarisation and the construction of failure. *British Educational Research Journal*, 26(5), 631–48.

CHRISTIANSEN, B. and WALTHER, G. (1986) Task and activity. In B. Christiansen, A. G. Howson and M. Otte (eds), *Perspectives on Mathematics Education*. Dordrecht: Reidel.

DfEE (1999) *The National Numeracy Strategy, Framework for Teaching Mathematics from Reception to Year Six*. Suffolk: DfEE Publications.

DOYLE, W. (1983) Academic Work. *Review of Educational Research*, 53, 159–99.

HOUSSART, J. (2001) Setting tasks and setting children. *Proceedings of the Fifth British Congress of Mathematics Education*, Keele University, 5–7 July.

LOW ATTAINERS IN MATHEMATICS PROJECT (1987) *Better Mathematics: A Curriculum Development Study*. London: HMSO.

MARGERISON, A. and RAYNER, S. (1999) Troubling targets and school needs: assessing behaviour in the classroom context. *Support for Learning*, 14(2), 87–92.

Ofsted (1998) *Setting in Primary Schools*. London: Ofsted Publications.

POLYA, G. (1966) On teaching problem solving. In Conference Board of Mathematical Sciences, *The Role of Axiomatics and Problem Solving in Mathematics*. Washington: Ginn and Co.

SHUARD, H. and ROTHERY, A. (1984) *Children Reading Mathematics*. London: John Murray.

SKEMP, R. (1979) *Intelligence, Learning and Action*. Chichester: John Wiley and Sons.

SUKHNANDAN, L. and LEE, B. (1998) *Streaming, Setting and Grouping by Ability. A review of the literature*. Slough: National Foundation for Educational Research.

TRICKETT, L. and SULKE, F. (1988) Low attainers can do mathematics. In D. Pimm (ed.), *Mathematics, Teachers and Children*. London: Hodder and Stoughton.

Possibilities

The following four chapters all offer possibilities for working with those who are getting low results in school and national assessments. The authors of these chapters all focus on the considerable thinking powers which all children display, given a suitable pedagogic and social environment in which to do so. The overarching belief is that children can learn more, think more effectively about mathematics, and construct complex understandings with the teacher's help. It is up to teachers to find ways to help them do this. This is in contrast to teaching approaches which intend to simplify, smooth or contextualise key mathematical concepts for lower attaining students. Unfortunately, like water, that which flows in easily can also flow out easily unless some real transforming work has been done by the learner. Transformation is only possible if a learner has some initial understanding with which to work. Hence, as Julia Anghileri points out (Chapter 9), formal written arithmetical methods are more efficiently and accurately used if they bear some relationship to the child's intuitive methods which may have been devised idiosyncratically to handle small numbers. Formal methods which are based on a more sophisticated knowledge, such as multiplicative number structure rather than additive, are more likely to lead to confusion, rejection of past confidence, and hence embed feelings of failure.

Tony Harries (Chapter 8) writes about some work in which children's thinking could be revealed and recorded using software. His particular example shows some low attaining students doing sophisticated thinking, creating new objects with which to develop more complex ideas. A more general observation would be that computers allow exploration in ways which are not offered by pencil and paper, and also offer evidence of thinking in ways which practical materials cannot offer. Thus a teacher, seeing the trickle files produced by these students, might learn that they are capable of complex construction of concepts and thus search for more ways to harness this capability in mathematics lessons.

In the third chapter in this group, Chapter 10, Rosalyn Hyde uses calculators to provide further exploratory and responsive learning environments. Inevitable questions arising for the learner are: How does it work? What can I do to make x happen? What will happen if I do? Why? An interactive engagement with mathematical structure arises from the technological tool; but the interaction is about mathematics, not the tool itself.

Finally in this group, Stephanie Prestage and Pat Perks describe a well-tried approach to teaching about algebraic expressions which allows all students to develop their understanding of the nature of expressions, their structure and the possibilities for use. The focus is on understanding, rather than doing, solving and manipulating. Like the other three chapters, what they offer seems to be topic-specific but is also an example of a generic approach to teaching. All four chapters are written by authors who expect all learners to achieve more if they are allowed and encouraged to work out their own understandings and use them to do more complex tasks.

CHAPTER 8

Working through complexity: an experience of developing mathematical thinking through the use of Logo with low attaining pupils

TONY HARRIES

Introduction

In this chapter I reflect on work undertaken with a group of low attaining pupils in Year 9 of an 11–18 comprehensive school. All the pupils in the study were assessed, by the school, as operating at level 2/3 of the National Curriculum for Mathematics. The study was developed in part to explore ways in which these pupils might be given access to algebraic ideas such as moving from the particular to the general through the use of variables within computer programming.

The data collected consisted of detailed case studies of eight pupils over a period of about nine months. It was gathered through interviews, task observation, a computerised record of all the key presses used during a session, and written assessments.

I consider one set of activities that the pupils undertook. These activities were called 'working with complex objects'. In order to put the work in context within this chapter, I will briefly explore the nature of low attainment, consider how the computer can act as a motivator within mathematics, describe the tasks and the pupil responses in detail and then reflect on the implications.

Background

In considering the nature of low attainment, the view taken in this chapter is that expressed by many of the Russian writers (see Krutetski, 1976), that ability is not fixed, and that all pupils possess the potential to develop their ability in mathematics. Having taken this position, a consideration of the factors that would facilitate the development of this ability is crucial. The study includes affective factors such as motivation and the development of a sense of curiosity. This relates to the work of Bruner (1970) and Vergnaud (1990), and emphasises the importance of the context and/or environment within which the pupil is learning. Interestingly, although the study is concerned with the work of low attaining pupils, there is a link with the work of Howe (1992) who, in his discussion on the development of gifted children, suggested that the children were not just 'naturally gifted' but that the environment in which they developed was one which aroused and encouraged curiosity. It was this deep sense of curiosity, he suggested, that played a large part in the astonishing learning of some of these children. Thus in developing work with low attaining pupils it was felt that the choice of environment was an important factor.

The nature of the mathematical entities with which the pupils in the study tended to work was considered within the context of a debate about the duality of process and object as developed by Sfard (1991), Tall (1993) and Douady (1985). Of these, Tall's work is possibly the most appropriate, as he developed the idea of a *procept* which brings the process and object aspects of a mathematical entity together with the way in which they are represented. In Logo we might get the following steps in working towards a proceptual way of thinking:

1. Small steps	2. Naming a sequence	3. Recognising structure	4. Focus on the object
Fd 100 rt 90 fd 100 rt 90 fd 100 rt 90 fd 100	To square Fd 100 rt 90 fd 100 rt 90 fd 100 rt 90 fd 100 end	To square Repeat 4 [fd 100 rt 90] end	Square
(a succession of small steps using primitive objects)	(naming a sequence of primitive objects)	(naming a sequence using an understanding of structure)	(focus on the object but with important Logo features noted – curser starts and ends at left-hand corner facing up screen)

When working in any symbolic system there will be primitive objects which can be operated on in order to create more complex objects. In order to progress efficiently within the symbolic system these objects will need to be viewed proceptually, otherwise the system becomes slow and cumbersome to manipulate. The work of Douady was felt to be important because of his consideration of the importance of context and the role of the teacher in helping the pupils to develop flexible and powerful ways of working with mathematical entities.

The environment chosen was Logo since it was considered that this environment was an appropriate one for helping pupils to construct mathematical meaning particularly related to the development of algebra (Hoyles and Sutherland, 1990; Sutherland, 1992). Access to the language was possible through the use of single primitive commands, and these commands could be combined to create procedures as shown above. In Logo a procedure is a named sequence of drawing commands which perform a subtask and which can be called upon by name when it is required to contribute to a more complex task. It was further felt that the use of appropriate tasks within this environment could help the pupils to construct meaning both individually and through social interaction. Thus they have the opportunity of working at both *inter* and *intra* psychological levels as appropriate (Vygotsky, 1978). The pupils worked in situations in which they used mathematical objects as discussed earlier; processes were performed both on and with these objects which had varying degrees of complexity. The objects with which the pupils worked were often themselves the result of processes performed on less complex objects. Thus one of the important ideas that was probed was the extent to which the pupils were able to work with the idea that mathematical entities could be both objects and processes.

The tasks

The pupils worked on two Logo-based activities about two months apart. They were given a set of procedures which drew shapes – a square, a line and a V – and a set of procedures which moved the drawing cursor in particular ways across the screen. Thus they had a set of objects with which to work. In order to complete the activities they needed to focus on both the process and object aspects of the procedures. In the first activity the procedures only contained numerical values for the lengths and the angles, whereas in the second the pupils had to input numerical values because the procedures used variables to represent generalisation. The objectives for the task were:

- to enable pupils to focus on a named procedure as an object that can be used in different contexts, and also as a process which defines the object
- to enable pupils to use named procedures as sub-procedures
- to enable pupils to manipulate objects (procedures) that are themselves processes.

In considering the work of the pupils at the computer, four ways of working emerged. These can be summarised on the grid below:

	Single step	Single step/complex object	Multiple step/complex object
Instant feedback	√	√	√
Delayed feedback			√

The first – *single step/instant feedback* – is demonstrated by Kerry and Kathy. They work almost exclusively in the graphic screen and use sequences of primitive commands which give instant feedback after each input. Their mode of working was almost exclusively a process mode using primitive objects which they sequenced in small steps. The fact that they were given a set of procedures to work with seemed to cause confusion and they were unable to use these procedures themselves and thus did not work at all with complex objects. They produced no designs for printing.

The second way of working – *single step with complex objects/instant feedback* – was demonstrated by Carol, Christine and Charlie. They tended to work first in the graphic screen and then, from notes, write complex procedures for their sequences of commands – including calling on the given procedures. Their style of working can be illustrated by the work of Charlie who worked initially in very much a process mode in that he worked in the graphic screen and treated the shape procedures as objects. He used them in the same way as he would the primitive commands and responded to the screen feedback which determined where the cursor was at any time. He worked with only two of the shapes as objects and seemed unable to view the move procedures as objects. The moves from one shape to the next were organised through a sequence of primitive commands. Once he had completed the first stick person he used the same structure to produce a set of pictures as in Figure 1. In each case he tested his work in the graphic screen, and decided if he was satisfied with the result or not.

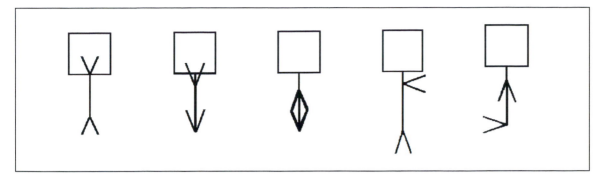

Figure 1. Charlie's designs

In the second activity he used numerical inputs to test the shape procedures in the graphic screen, but avoided some which required more than one input. Then, having organised the sequence of commands in the graphic screen he named the sequence – Q. This was followed by use of a repeat command, e.g. repeat 100 [Q rt 10], which means repeat the sequence inside the square bracket 100 times. The use of letters in the procedures given did not cause him any confusion and he worked with the idea systematically (see Figure 2).

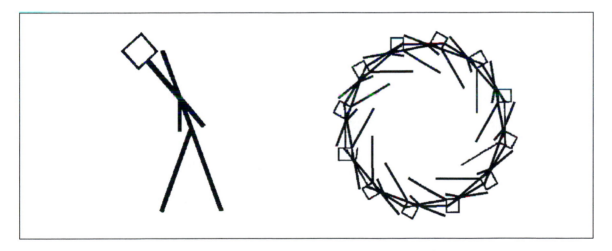

Figure 2. Charlie's second set of designs

The resulting diagram provides an interesting illustration of the importance of knowing how a procedure is built up, since the actual diagram looks as if it represents 'Repeat 12 [Q lt 30]'. The crucial factor is knowing where the drawing cursor ends up at the end of the procedure Q (on the square) and where the drawing of the next Q starts (on the V of the legs). For Charlie, the shape procedures were by their very nature tangible objects that it was logical to name. They were treated as objects whose size could be chosen by means of an appropriate input. The moves, however, are physically dynamic and so to see them as objects would appear to be difficult. These commands were not used at all.

The third way of working – *multiple step and complex object/instant feedback* – was demonstrated by Steve, who worked on both the design and his complex procedure simultaneously. He would write a named sequence for part of the design and after testing would add it to his procedure. Thus he would build up the graphic object and the symbolic object together. In this way he was working simultaneously on both the process and object aspect of the procedure that he was building. The natures of both the move procedures and the shape procedures were explored using a variety of inputs. This gave him a feel for what the shape looked like and how the inputs affected the size. Having identified the nature of the given procedures, he tested his ideas in the graphic screen to produce his own figure (Figure 3).

Figure 3. Steve's design

The first procedure did not give the required design and so he abandoned the procedure and started again. This time he worked in a slightly different way in that he built his procedure 'bit by bit' and tested each bit as he went along – thus going back to instant feedback. He then edited his procedure on the basis of the visual feedback received from the graphic screen. In working on this activity, Steve is working at two levels. Firstly he is working towards the creation of a visual object, and secondly he is simultaneously working towards the creation of a symbolic object – the procedure which will produce the picture. Thus he would seem to be working on both the process and the object nature of the design in both environments.

The fourth way of working – *multiple step and complex object/delayed feedback* – is demonstrated by Lucy and Simon, who would plan away from the computer and would have a clear idea of their intended design before starting to work at the keyboard. At the keyboard they would sometimes work first in the graphic screen and then write the named procedure, and at other times they would start by writing a procedure and then test it on the graphic screen. They were very conscious of the need to know the underlying process for each of the given procedures, and their style of working would vary – sometimes concentrating on processes using the primitive and the complex objects and at other times concentrating on the creation of new objects through working in the editor. Lucy's work illustrates this style of working. Away from the computer Lucy sketched each of the given procedures – thus accentuating the process aspect of the objects with which she would work. Having completed this she typed in all the procedures given and thus built up all the named procedures/objects for herself. Thus in exploring the given complex objects she has moved from a symbolic object to the process which the object represents. Having created a sequence using the given objects in the graphic screen she then created and named a new complex procedure, 'TWO'. This was undertaken in short stages where the addition of a new command was tested in the graphic screen. In this way the final procedure was created. It would seem that the process and object aspects of the procedures are closely linked and that further, the visual and symbolic representations are also linked (see Figure 4).

Figure 4. Lucy's design

In the second activity, where the procedures contained variables, Lucy's approach showed more confidence in working in the Logo environment. Each of the shape and move procedures was explored using a variety of inputs. She was thus able to explore the nature of the given objects without focusing on the process by which they were derived. These complex objects were used to create a sequence of commands in the graphic screen with the visual feedback addressing the process aspects of the procedure. Thus her approach here is different from that used in the previous activity in that she starts to build up through drawing an acceptable sequence which is named as a procedure and which is then checked on the graphic screen (see Figure 5).

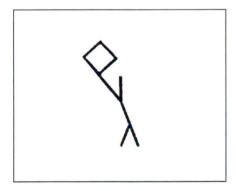

Figure 5. Lucy's second design

Discussion

In discussing the object/process duality of mathematical entities, Tall (1996) rightly suggests that:

> . . . it is not only the things that pupils can do that measure progress, but how they do them and whether their methods can be built on in subsequent development.

He goes on to suggest that those who are successful at mathematics have a range of facts that they use flexibly to create derived facts whereas the least successful have a limited range of facts which they use with little flexibility. There is another element which was important for the pupils in the study, and that was the meaning which they were able to attach to what they did and how they did it. The meaning was directly related to the objects with which they worked and the processes they were able to perform on the objects. In some of the work illustrated above, the following were evident: the notion of primitive objects; operations on primitive objects which give rise to complex objects; and then operations on the complex objects. The evidence from the case studies highlights the object/process duality and the difficulty that these low attaining pupils have in thinking about and using the duality effectively.

The symbol systems used in Logo to represent the objects with which they worked and the processes being undertaken were significant. In particular, in using the symbolic system embedded within Logo a familiarity with the various ways in which symbols were used needed to be developed by the pupils. There were given symbols for primitive objects, pupil-created symbols for complex objects, pupil-created symbols to represent parts of the processes that were carried out on the primitive and complex objects, and finally there were pupil-created symbols to represent undetermined parts (and relationships on these) of the objects being used.

In the full study (Harries, 1997) the same phenomena were observed within various areas of working mathematically (see Figure 6). The pupils worked with a number of *primitive objects*. With these primitive objects they did not need to consider the underlying process aspect of the object – how it was created – and used them as entities on which operations were performed. They were entities which they did not need to break down any further. On these primitive objects *simple processes*, such as adding, subtracting or sequencing, were performed in order to create new and more complex objects with which they could work further. Similarly, complex processes could be performed on the primitive objects. In the areas of number, algebra and within the Logo environment the objects and operations would be characterised as below:

Aspect	Primitive objects	Simple processes	Complex processes
Number	Small numbers	Simple addition Simple subtraction	Multiplication as repeated addition Division as repeated subtraction Combined operations such as double and add 1 . . .
Logo	Primitive commands	Simple sequences Naming the sequence	Complex sequences such as using Repeat Using previously named sequences
Algebra	Symbols which represent undetermined values of specific quantities	Simple relationships such as $x + 1$, $x/10$ . . .	Combined operations such as $2x + 1$ or $x + y$ . . .

Figure 6. Objects and processes within number, Logo and algebra

Similar styles of working were observed with these pupils, whether they were working arithmetically, algebraically or in Logo. In the Logo work the pupils were all able to use the primitive commands (fd . . . , rt . . .) in named sequences to create complex objects. The difficulty arose when using these new objects since they needed to be aware of their dual nature in order to use them appropriately.

It is important now to try to identify the new power that the pupils gain from working in a way which focuses attention on the objects within a problem and not just the processes involved. The main difference observed was that of developing reasoning. The Logo work had an influence here in that the whole exercise of de-bugging procedures depends on focusing on and asking questions about the objects in a procedure. This involves reasoning and asking questions such as 'Why did this happen?' and 'What can I do to stop this happening?'

In particular, in the tasks discussed above, most of the pupils were able to advance beyond ways of working which used primitive objects and ways of operating on them – counting in single digits, using single direct drive commands in Logo – to using more complex objects as their starting points, such as a named procedure in Logo. The environment motivated the pupils to seek new starting points in order that their work became more efficient and that they did not have to start each session from the same initial position. (It is recognised that the learning environment consists of a number of interrelated elements: the tasks with which the pupils engage, pupil interaction with each other and with the teacher while working on the tasks, and Logo itself.)

The results of the study suggest that most of these low attaining pupils can work with both complex objects and basic algebraic ideas when presented in a Logo context. The use of a language such as Logo provided the pupils with an environment in which they could experience the object/process duality of mathematical entities and some important ideas central to the development of algebra.

The results suggest that, given appropriate tasks, these pupils are able to engage in algebraic activity and give meaning to algebraic concepts. Further, there is evidence that prior knowledge of algebraic-type symbolism is not a prerequisite for work using the algebraic symbolism of Logo and becoming proficient in the use of the language.

It would seem that an approach needs to be developed which helps the pupils to build a range of objects with which they can work and to which they are able to attach meaning. This would help the pupils to develop a parallel interpretation of mathematical entities as both objects and processes – an interpretation that Tall (1996) suggests is a distinguishing feature of the work of pupils who do well at mathematics and those who struggle with it.

Further, there would seem to be an implication that the curriculum for these pupils should not be restricted by preconceived ideas about what the pupils might be capable of absorbing. There is a need for the creation of problem-solving situations both at and away from the computer which allow the pupils to give meaning to the concepts on which they are focusing. Increasing the range of these situations allows the pupils to build stronger understanding of the concepts being developed. The concentration on mechanical manipulations, which is often a feature of the mathematics given to low attaining pupils, has the effect of restricting the meaning that pupils are able to give to such manipulations, and focuses attention on processes and not on the creation of complex objects which can ease the manipulation.

References

BRUNER, J. S. (1970) Some theorems on instruction. In E. Stones (ed.), *Readings in Educational Psychology*. London: Methuen.

DOUADY, R. (1985) The interplay between different settings: Tool–object dialect in the extension of mathematical ability – examples from elementary school teaching. In *Proceedings of the Ninth International Conference for the Psychology of Mathematics Education*, Vol. 2, pp. 33–52. Utrecht: State University of Utrecht.

HARRIES, A. V. (1997) *Developing Algebra Concepts with Low Attainers Working in a Logo Environment*. Unpublished PhD thesis, University of Bristol, School of Education.

HOWE, M. J. A. (1992) *The Origins of Exceptional Ability*. Oxford: Basil Blackwell.

HOYLES, C. and SUTHERLAND, R. (1990) Logo: an aid to pupils' thinking and learning.

In H. Mandl, E. de Corte, S. N. Bennett and H. F. Friedrich (eds), *Learning and Instruction,* 2(1), pp. 411–26. Oxford: Pergamon Press.

KRUTETSKI, V. A. (1976) *The Psychology of Mathematical Abilities in School Children.* Chicago: University of Chicago Press.

SFARD, A. (1991) On the dual nature of mathematical conceptions: reflections on processes and objects as different sides of the same coin. *Educational Studies in Mathematics,* 22, 1–36.

SUTHERLAND, R. (1992) What is algebraic about programming in Logo? In C. Hoyles and R. Noss (ed.), *Learning Mathematics and Logo,* Boston: MIT Press, 37–54.

TALL, D. (1993) The transition from arithmetic to algebra: number patterns or proceptual programming. *Proceedings of Second Annual Conference on Teaching and Learning.* London.

TALL, D. (1996) Can all children climb the same curriculum ladder? Plenary Lecture. *Proceedings of the Eighth International Conference on Mathematics Education,* Spain.

VERGNAUD, G. (1990) Problem-solving and concept formation in the learning of mathematics. In H. Mandl, E. de Corte, S. N. Bennett and H. F. Friedrich (eds), *Learning and Instruction,* 2(2). Oxford: Pergamon Press.

VYGOTSKY, L. S. (1978) *Mind in Society.* Cambridge, MA: Harvard University Press.

CHAPTER 9

A study of progression in written calculation strategies for division

JULIA ANGHILERI

Reform of the mathematics curriculum has led to a shift in teaching arithmetic from the repetition and rehearsal of standard written procedures to a focus on developing children's own approaches. Children today are expected to observe patterns and relationships so that they understand connections among the different numbers and operations, and develop a 'feel' for numbers often referred to as 'number sense'. The term 'number sense' is widely used across the world in reform documents (NCTM, 1989; AEC, 1991) and refers to 'flexibility' and 'inventiveness' in strategies for calculating as a reaction to overemphasis on the computational procedures that have been taught in the past that were devoid of thinking. Pupils today are expected to understand the calculation methods that they use in a way that contrasts starkly with past expectations. For pupils with special educational needs this can be both an opportunity, as their thinking about problems is respected, but also an added pressure as it can be difficult to understand the compact standard methods. In the past, understanding was not required. This is made clear in the following quote from a section entitled 'Over-explanation of processes to duller pupils':

> . . . what they need to know is how to get the sum right, and when they have learned the method so thoroughly that the possibilities of getting the particular type of sum wrong are only the ordinary ones due to chance, then explanations might be attempted . . . Why should we burden children with unnecessary explanations in arithmetic?
>
> (Schonell, 1937, p. 73)

Reflecting current expectations, the UK *Framework for Teaching Mathematics from Reception to Year 6* uses the term 'numeracy' to identify 'the proficiency in number that involves a confidence and competence with numbers requiring an understanding of the number system, a repertoire of computational skills and an inclination and ability to solve number problems in a variety of contexts' (DfEE, 1998). The National Curriculum reinforces the importance of flexibility in approaches to calculations requiring 'efficient written methods' rather than *standard* written methods and notes that 'pupils are expected to use mental methods if the calculations are suitable' (DfEE, 1999, p. 23).

Number sense involves a way of thinking that enables children to identify important relationships quickly, for example, that 48 is not only the same as '40 + 8', but also that it is '50 – 2' and 'double 24' and '6 eights'. The way numbers relate to each other, the possibilities for different representations, and the meanings that can be associated with the different operations, will all play a key role in establishing the connections that are crucial in developing number sense.

> Number sense refers to a person's general understanding of number and operations along with the ability and inclination to use this understanding in flexible ways to make mathematical judgements and to develop useful strategies for handling numbers and operations.
>
> (Mcintosh, Reys and Reys, 1992)

It has become important for teachers and learning support assistants to recognise the limitations inherent in standardised procedures for calculating, and to identify and build on the sense that individuals make of different problems. Errors and misconceptions may be identified more readily through informal and idiosyncratic working; addressing such problems is an important element of the National Numeracy Strategy (DfEE, 1998).

Justification for changes in teaching number

The justification for the move away from an emphasis on standard written procedures lies partly in the fact that in the workplace 'human calculators', who are well practised in standard methods (such as multiplying and dividing fractions, and long division), are no longer required (Shuard, Walsh, Goodwin and Worcester, 1991). It is more important to be able to apply concepts to settings which are not immediately familiar, such as problems which are not exact repetitions of exercises (Schoenfeld, 1988). In today's society, powerful technical aids are available to assist with the laborious aspects of calculations, enabling people to develop and use mathematical understanding that is relevant to different complexities in problem-solving (Noss, 1999).

It is not only the development of powerful technical aids that has brought about a need to address the purpose of mathematics teaching. Theories of learning developed in the last century by psychologists have questioned the effectiveness of a 'transmission'-based model for learning, with emphasis on 'drill and practice', and research has shown limitations in the success of such approaches (Skemp, 1976; Askew, Brown, Rhodes, William and Johnson, 1997). More recent theories of how children learn mathematics have come to be termed 'constructivist' (von Glasersfeld, 1991) and are based on the view that mathematical knowledge is constructed by the learners themselves as they seek out meanings and make mental connections in an active manner. It has therefore become increasingly important to access children's own thinking about problems and their solution. This will enable teachers and adult supporters to build on the understanding that is evident and to address any misconceptions that may have developed. It will also be helpful to analyse progression from naive intuitive methods to more efficient written strategies and to consider the influence of teaching on this development.

Progressing from naive approaches

When children are viewed as the constructors of their own knowledge their intuitive understanding forms the foundations upon which further understanding is built. Pupils' own approaches will often begin with naive strategies involving literal interpretations and inefficient solution methods (Fischbein, Deri, Nello and Marino, 1985; Anghileri, 1998). With early success using these strategies, some children will be reluctant to progress to more complex methods which may seem more abstract and remote from the problems to be solved. In the current curriculum in schools, children are encouraged to develop mental strategies in problem-solving and to use informal jottings to support their thinking where the numbers are large. This focus on the pupils' own thinking has the benefit of encouraging autonomy in tackling problems, but if personal confidence is to be maintained there needs to be a progressive process of negotiation as more formal calculation methods are introduced. The gap between children's informal approaches and the standardised procedures of the written algorithms presents a challenge for teachers and adult supporters who must guide the development of strategies to increase efficiency without loss of understanding. Thompson (1997) proposes a progression in addition and subtraction calculations using expanded written formats that reflect children's mental strategies before progressing to the compact standard methods. Expanded written formats are also suggested in guidance for teachers (QCA, 1999), but it is not always clear how more formal methods can be introduced as a development of the pupils' own thinking. This paper reports a study to clarify the progression from naive approaches to more formal written methods for the operation of division of whole numbers.

The operation of division

The operation of division presents more complexities than addition and subtraction, not only because there are two distinct procedures represented by the operation, but also because most calculation methods require the knowledge of multiplication facts and the ability to estimate as well as to use addition or subtraction within the solution. Division is first introduced in school as a formalisation of sharing, and this model holds an enduring position in pupils' intuitive thinking (Fischbein et al., 1985). Although this serves as one possible model, an equally powerful interpretation relates division to finding the number of equal groups in a given total. These two models, referred to as *partitive* division and *quotitive* division, form the basis for analysing the operation for whole numbers (Greer, 1992). Pupils' solution procedures have been associated with the resulting different structures of word problems, but more recent findings suggest that children have different sets of intuitive models (direct counting, repeated addition/subtraction, and multiplicative approaches) that they apply to division problems (Murray, Olivier and Human, 1991; Mulligan and Mitchelmore, 1997). For developing efficiency, such interpretations cannot be ignored as they represent the pupils' thinking in a way that more formal methods do not. Some researchers (for example, Kouba, 1989) suggest that there is no direct correspondence between the structure of a problem and the method a child uses to solve it. Children become able to select a method independent of the problem type but which best suits the numbers (Clarke and Kamii, 1996). Although children initially develop powerful non-standard algorithms alongside school-taught standard algorithms (Murray et al., 1991), these can be devalued where conciseness becomes an issue and where there is a requirement for standard procedures to be taught.

Difficulties arise where the procedure for the traditional algorithm is incompatible with intuitive approaches (Anghileri and Beishuizen, 1998). For division, the more formal structure of formal written methods makes them prone to errors (Brown and

VanLehn, 1980) and without understanding of these methods children are unable to reconstruct the steps they cannot remember. Ruthven and Chaplin (1998) refer to 'the improvisation of malgorithms' to describe pupils' inappropriate adaptations of the procedures for the algorithm. Complexities arise when the values of the numbers appear to be less relevant, as pupils are taught a procedure for working with the digits and the meaning of the steps involved are not immediately clear. In order to tackle $7\overline{)98}$, for example, one starts by noting that '7 divided into 9' gives '1' which is the 'tens' part of the answer and the remainder of 2 becomes 20 units. This is a shorthand for '7 divided into 90 gives 10 with 20 remaining' (Anghileri, 2000), but does not easily relate to the calculation 'How many 7s are in 90?'

The research project

In order to understand the development in children's thinking from intuitive interpretations of division problems to use of more compact written calculation strategies, a study was undertaken to analyse the methods children used and the way these changed over time. By looking for progression in the development of strategies, teachers and LSAs can be better prepared to extend the understanding of pupils experiencing difficulties by introducing stages that build on intuitive attempts. It is usual for pupils at the age of nine to ten years to meet more formal written methods for division. In the UK this will normally involve the introduction of the traditional algorithm for short division by a single-digit divisor. This method may be introduced at different times in the school year with variations between schools and sometimes between children in the same class. Alternative approaches are used in the Netherlands where most Groep 4 (Year 5) children are taught division by one- and two-digit divisors as a whole class in the later part of the school year. The Dutch method uses an algorithm built on developed efficiency in repeated subtraction and will be the same for one- and two-digit divisors. It is usual in the Dutch approach to introduce large numbers to justify the change from informal and mental approaches to more formal written methods (Beishuizen and Anghileri, 1998).

The study involved Year 5 pupils in ten English schools (n = 279) chosen for the schools' overall high achievement in national tests (Key Stage 2 SATs results above the national average). It also involved Groep 4 (Year 5) pupils in ten Dutch schools (n = 256), selected because they all used textbooks that implemented a reform programme of Realistic Mathematics Education (Treffers and Beishuizen, 1999). The schools were in comparable English and Dutch 'university cities' and complete classes were tested. Ten division problems were written in identical format for each cohort, and pupils were asked to record all their working, showing the ways they 'thought about' solving each problem. Five of the problems were presented in word format with a context relating to sharing (*partition*) or to grouping (*quotition*). Five were 'bare' problems involving similar numbers but presented in symbols (see Table 1).

The numbers were chosen to invite connections to be made to children's existing knowledge of numbers (for example 64 ÷ 16 involved related numbers) and the problems resulted in some exact calculations and some remainders. Although division by a two-digit divisor is not usually introduced in the English curriculum in Year 5, the numbers were chosen so that informal methods could be used and intuitive approaches recorded. Children worked individually, with assistance in reading the problems where necessary, and were presented with the same calculations on two occasions, in January

Context problem	Bare problem
1. 98 flowers are bundled in bunches of 7. How many bunches can be made?	6. 96 ÷ 6
2. 64 pencils have to be packed in boxes of 16. How many boxes will be needed?	7. 84 ÷ 14
3. 432 children have to be transported by 15-seater buses. How many buses will be needed?	8. 538 ÷ 15
4. 604 blocks are laid down in rows of 10. How many rows will there be?	9. 804 ÷ 10
5. 1256 apples are divided among 6 shopkeepers. How many apples will each shopkeeper get? How many apples will be left?	10. 1542 ÷ 5

Table 1. Ten problems used in the first test

and in June of the same year. By analysing the calculation strategies at two points in the school year, changes could be characterised. In the second test the numerical problems and contexts were the same but numbers 'in context' and 'bare' problems were interchanged. By comparing English and Dutch children's solutions, developments in approach could be identified and the effectiveness of different teaching approaches considered.

Analysis of the solution strategies

With working space provided on the worksheets and encouragement given to the children to show their working, it was possible to collect and classify a large range of strategies used by the children. Some were naive and long-winded but effective for the problems where the numbers were not too large. The most concise methods were standardised procedures (algorithms) that had been taught to the children. In the Dutch children's solutions there was more evidence of a progression from naive to formal methods, with written recording that took account of this development. The English children's solution methods appear to show discontinuity between the naive approaches and the formal algorithm.

Naive methods including tallying (Figure 1a) and sharing (Figure 1b) were evident among both cohorts in the first test.

Such methods displayed an understanding of the problem and show the way the children were thinking about the problem, but were not always sustainable without errors.

Progression was evident through repeated addition or subtraction of the divisor (Figure 2). The repeated subtraction of the Dutch children was often recorded as a standardised procedure that would form the basis for more efficient methods.

The process of 'chunking' – using multiples of the divisor – led to different levels of efficiency gains and was evident in sharing procedures (Figure 3a) as well as in more structured calculations (Figure 3b).

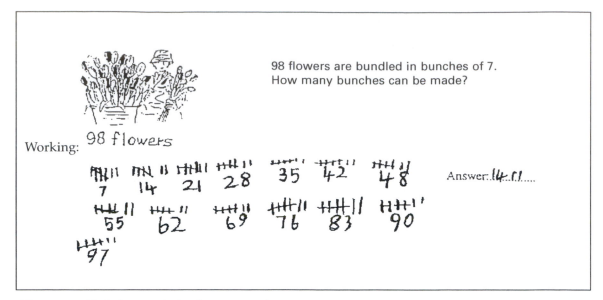

Figure 1a. Tallying and sharing strategies

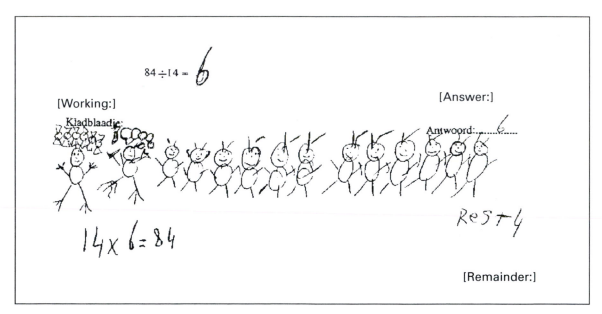

Figure 1b. Tallying and sharing strategies

Where the numbers were large and the chunks were small, this strategy could be long-winded and prone to errors in calculating. Where multiples of the divisor were chosen to produce a more efficient method, recording was varied. Recording by the English children was generally informal (Figure 4a) except where the traditional algorithm was used. The written recording of the Dutch children was generally more structured (Figure 4b) as they are taught a single method that allows different stages in the development of efficiency. It is noteworthy that this method allows for variation in choosing the 'chunks' to be subtracted and will still be effective for different choices. This gives autonomy to the learner and allows gradual progression to more efficiency without loss of understanding.

In contrast, the formal written method taught to the English children did not appear to relate well to their informal strategies. The formal written method most widely used by the English children was the traditional 'bus shelter' algorithm, and there were many errors in its use. The problem 1256 ÷ 6, for example, led to the answer 29 r 2, where the zero was missed out (Figure 5a). Where the algorithm was attempted for

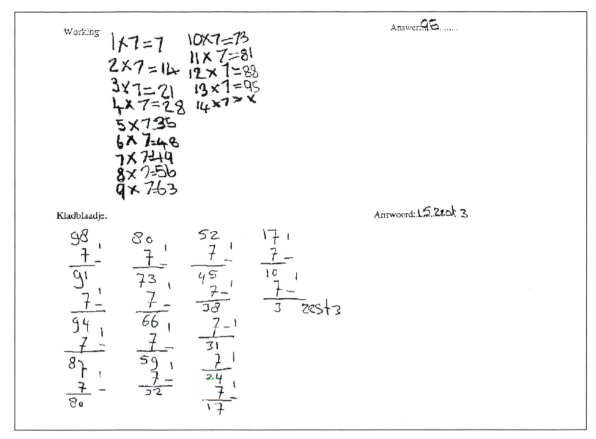

Figure 2. *Low level strategies*

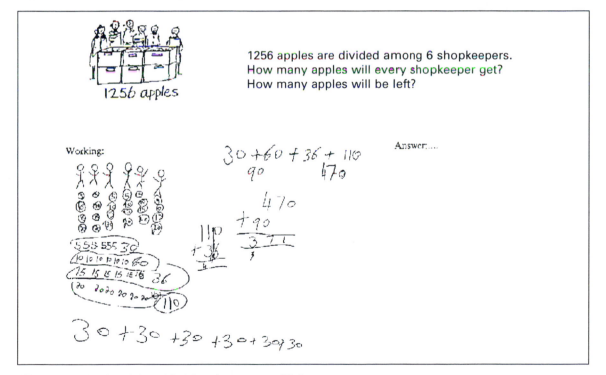

Figure 3a. *Using 'chunking' to improve efficiency*

problems with a two-digit divisor, for example 64 ÷ 16, inappropriate generalisations appeared to reflect procedures that had been learned for multiplication (first divide the tens and then the units) (Figures 5b and 5d). In some cases quite bizarre answers were given, suggesting that the calculations had been performed with no attempt to make any sense of the meanings (Figure 5c). In the example shown it appears that the

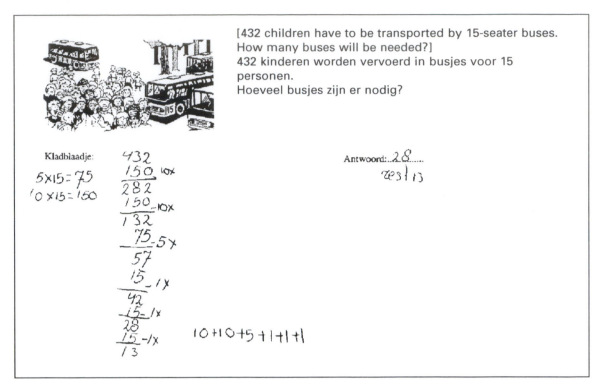

Figure 3b. Using 'chunking' to improve efficiency

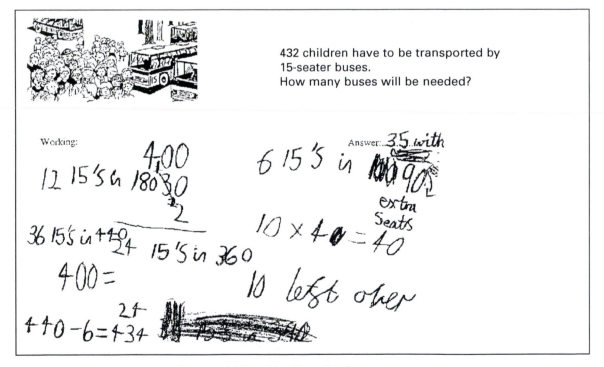

Figure 4a. Different recordings of 'chunking' methods

calculation starts with '6 into 12 goes once with 6 remaining'. From this initial correct but inappropriate estimate, it appears that the situation becomes impossible for the pupil to retrieve.

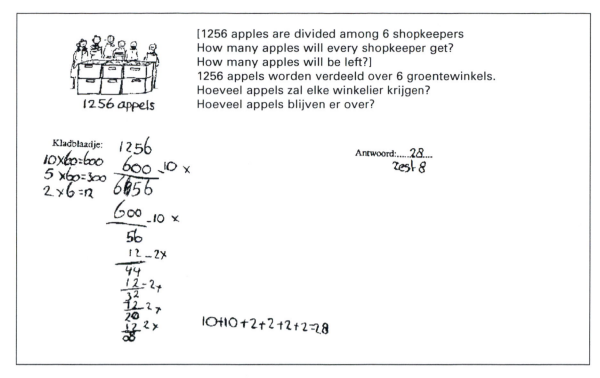

Figure 4b. *Different recordings of 'chunking' methods*

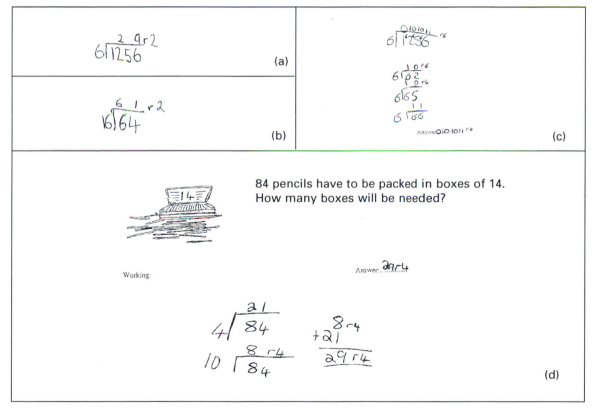

Figure 5. *Errors with the traditional algorithm*

Results

Overall success rates for the ten problems were similar for the English (38%) and the Dutch (47%) children in the first test in January. By June, in the second test, the Dutch achieved greater success (68%) than the English (44%), with the Dutch success rate greater than the English in every question. The lowest Dutch achievement in the second test was 53% correct for each of the problems 432 ÷ 15 and 538 ÷ 15. The English children had difficulty with these problems, achieving only 13% and 20% success, respectively, in the second test.

Since division by a two-digit divisor is not normally introduced in English classrooms in Year 5, the problems involving a single-digit divisor are considered separately. For both the English and the Dutch cohorts, the context problems were generally solved more successfully than the parallel bare problems (Table 2).

Test 1 January	98 ÷ 7 (context)	96 ÷ 6 (bare)	1256 ÷ 6 (context)	1542 ÷ 5 (bare)
English	62%	55%	20%	28%
Dutch	73%	62%	27%	27%
Test 2 June	96 ÷ 6 (context)	98 ÷ 7 (bare)	1542 ÷ 5 (context)	1256 ÷ 6 (bare)
English	73%	67%	37%	22%
Dutch	84%	81%	63%	56%

Table 2. Success rates for division by a single digit

The greatest difference in performance between the English and the Dutch children is seen in the second test in the results for the problems 1256 ÷ 6 and 1542 ÷ 5. These two problems were tackled successfully by more Dutch children (56% and 63% respectively) than by English children (22% and 37% respectively). For the four problems involving a single-digit divisor, more English pupils used naive strategies such as tallying and simple addition (6% in test 2) while fewer Dutch children persisted with such inefficient methods (1% in test 2). In the second test the most widely used strategies used by the Dutch children (in 74% of all attempts) involved high level chunking, often in a structured format for repeated subtraction. This latter strategy was successful in 81% of these attempts. The English algorithm was the most frequently used strategy by the English children, being used in 67% of attempts for these four problems. This was successful in 80% of the attempts for 98 ÷ 7 and 96 ÷ 6, but only successful in 40% of attempts for the other two problems. Where the English children had difficulties using the algorithm they appeared unable to revert to a more intuitive strategy for solving the problem, even when the numbers invited connections to be made.

Discussion

The extensive use of the traditional algorithm by English children in this study suggests that they do not develop informal methods that introduce efficiency without losing the general nature of their solution strategies. The better success of the Dutch children appears to relate to their use of a procedure that works at many levels of efficiency, and to the way even their naive attempts are structured by written recording. The Dutch approach, with repeated subtraction of 'chunks', will be effective for any choices, while a wrong first estimate in the English algorithm makes recovery and completion of the calculation very difficult.

Written calculation methods for division problems appear to be most successful where there is progressive development, with structured recording built on the more intuitive approaches that children initially use for calculations with small numbers. In contrast, the traditional algorithm most widely used by the English children appears to be detached from their more informal approaches as well as being prone to errors.

The informal strategies used for division may not be efficient, but do reveal the way children are thinking about the problems. Although methods such as tallying and repeated addition will not be appropriate for large numbers, as they are prone to errors in the calculations, they are clearly evident in some children's working at Year 5 and show the basis upon which more efficient strategies need to be built. Even where the numbers were very large, these methods were more evident among the English children in the study reported above and reflect the influence of the problem context in determining a solution strategy (Figure 6).

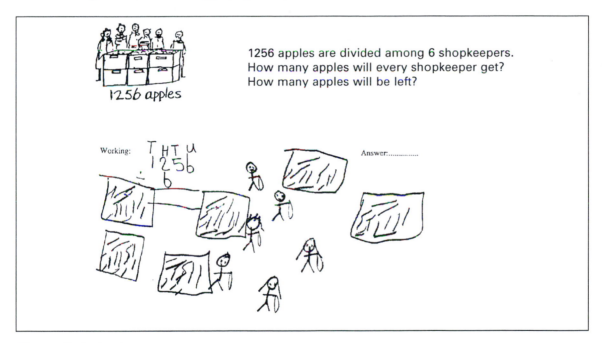

Figure 6. A sharing strategy

Children using these methods are demonstrating their understanding of the problems and it can be helpful for a teacher or LSA to recognise this as a sound starting point for calculating. In order to develop more reliable methods, efficiency gains that build on this understanding need to be introduced progressively. Where the procedure of sharing is used to reflect the semantic structure of the problem, for example, efficiency gains may be achieved by sharing larger chunks.

References

AEC (AUSTRALIAN EDUCATION COUNCIL) (1991) *A National Statement on Mathematics for Australian Schools*. Carlton, Victoria: Curriculum Corporation.

ANGHILERI, J. (1998) A discussion of different approaches to arithmetic teaching. In A. Olivier and K. Newstead (eds), *Proceedings of the Twenty-second International Conference for the Psychology of Mathematics Education*, Vol. 2, 2–17.

ANGHILERI, J. (2000) *Teaching Number Sense*. London: Continuum.

ANGHILERI, J. and BEISHUIZEN, M. (1998) Counting, chunking and the division algorithm. *Mathematics in School*, 27, 1.

ASKEW, M., BROWN, M., RHODES, V., WILIAM, D. and JOHNSON, D. (1997) *Effective Teachers of Numeracy: Report of a study carried out for the Teacher Training Agency*. London: King's College, University of London.

BEISHUIZEN, M. and ANGHILERI, J. (1998) Which mental strategies in the early number curriculum? *British Education Research Journal*, 24, 5.

BROWN, J. and VAN LEHN, K. (1980) Repair theory: a generative theory of bugs in procedural skills. *Cognitive Science*, 4, 379–426.

CLARKE, F. and KAMII, C. (1996) Identification of multiplicative thinking in children in grades 1–5. *Journal for Research in Mathematics Education*, 27(1), 41–51.

DfEE (1998) *Implementation of the National Numeracy Strategy: Final report of the Numeracy Task Force*. London: DfEE.

DfEE (1999a) *Mathematics: The National Curriculum for England*. London: DfEE.

DfEE (1999b) *National Numeracy Strategy, Framework for Teaching Mathematics from Reception to Year 6*. London: DfEE.

FISCHBEIN, E., DERI, M., NELLO, M. and MARINO, M. (1985) The role of implicit models in solving verbal problems in multiplication and division. *Journal for Research in Mathematics Education*, 16, 3–17.

GREER, B. (1992) Multiplication and division as models of situations. In D. Grouws (ed.), *Handbook of Research on Mathematics Teaching and Learning*. New York: Macmillan, 276–95.

KOUBA, V. (1989) Children's solution strategies for equivalent set multiplication and division word problems. *Journal for Research in Mathematics Education*, 20, 147–58.

McINTOSH, A., REYS, B. and REYS, R. (1992) A proposed framework for examining number sense. *For the Learning of Mathematics*, 12(3), 2–8.

MULLIGAN, J. and MITCHELMORE, M. (1997) Young children's intuitive models of multiplication and division. *Journal for Research in Mathematics Education*, 28(3), 309–30.

MURRAY, H., OLIVIER, A. and HUMAN, P. (1991) Young children's division strategies. In F. Furinghetti (ed.), *Proceedings of the Fifteenth International Conference for the Psychology of Mathematics Education*, Vol. 3. Assissi, Italy, 49–56.

NCTM (NATIONAL COUNCIL FOR TEACHERS OF MATHEMATICS) (1989) *Curriculum and Evaluation Standards for School Mathematics*. Reston, Va: NCTM.

NOSS, R. (1999) New numeracies for a technological culture. *For the Learning of Mathematics*, 18(2), 2–12.

QCA (1999) *Teaching Written Calculation Strategies*. London: QCA.

RUTHVEN, K. and CHAPLIN, D. (1997) The calculator as a cognitive tool: upper-primary pupils tackling a realistic number problem. *International Journal of Computers for Mathematical Learning*, 2(2), 93–124.

SCHOENFELD, A. H. (1988) When good teaching leads to bad results: the disasters of 'well-taught' mathematics courses. *Educational Psychologist*, 23, 145–66.

SCHONELL, F. (1937) *Diagnosis of Individual Difficulties in Arithmetic*. London: Oliver and Boyd.

SHUARD, H., WALSH, A., GOODWIN, G. and WORCESTER, V. (1991) *Calculators, Children and Mathematics*. London: Simon and Schuster for the National Curriculum Council.

SKEMP, R. (1976) Relational understanding and instrumental understanding. *Mathematics Teaching*, 77, 20–6.

THOMPSON, I. (1997) Mental and written algorithms: can the gap be bridged? In I. Thompson (ed.), *Teaching and Learning Early Number*. Buckingham: Open University Press.

TREFFERS, A. and BEISHUIZEN, M. (1999) Realistic mathematics education in the Netherlands. In I. Thompson (ed.), *Issues in Teaching Numeracy in Primary Schools*. Buckingham: Open University Press.

VON GLASERSFELD, E. (ed.) (1991) *Radical Constructivism in Mathematics Education*. Dordrecht: Kluwer Academic Publishers.

CHAPTER 10

Using graphics calculators with low attaining pupils

ROSALYN HYDE

Introduction

There is a long history of graphics calculator use in schools and colleges in the United Kingdom. Generally, this technology has been used with older or higher attaining students in Key Stages 4 and 5, rather than low attaining students of any age. The introduction of the Key Stage 3 Strategy for mathematics in September 2001 has led to increased interest in the use of graphics calculators with younger pupils, and there has also been recent small-scale activity where teachers have been using this technology with pupils in Years 5 and 6. However, it is likely that this technology is still largely used only with higher attaining students. The contention here is that there is much for low attaining pupils to gain from using graphics calculators, and that this technology can help to support the learning of these pupils.

The place of hand-held technology

The use of hand-held technology is firmly rooted in the provision of ICT within mathematics and is clearly seen as having a role in enhancing the teaching and learning of mathematics. This is demonstrated in three publications from BECTa (1999; 2000; 2001). The influence of these documents can clearly be seen in the *Framework for Teaching Mathematics: Years 7, 8 and 9* (DfEE, 2001) section on ICT (p. 25). This framework contains many suggestions for using a graphics calculator with pupils across the attainment targets, and graphics calculators are listed as one of the main uses of ICT in mathematics at Key Stage 3 (DfEE, 2001, p. 25).

Benefits of using the technology

This technology offers a number of advantages over computers. In particular it offers:

- portability
- accessibility
- integration into normal classroom practice
- flexibility
- low cost.

Graphics calculators also offer pupils access to instant personal feedback on their work, the opportunity to conjecture and to test those conjectures, and opportunities to visualise and interact with visually constructed models of mathematics. Ruthven (1994, p. 155) says that that graphics calculators can become a 'genuinely personal tool for individual students'. These are also tools that support pupils in making links in mathematics: linking numeric, graphic and symbolic representations (Ruthven, 1994, p. 162; Smith, 2002), between areas of mathematics, and across the curriculum with the use of data loggers. Barbour and Bethel (1995) note that this is technology that is made for the mathematics classroom and mathematics learning more generally.

Smith (2002) suggests four ways in which using graphics calculators can enrich the learning experiences of pupils. He says that graphics calculators can be used as:

1. tools for expediency in reducing the time and effort required to perform cumbersome mathematical tasks
2. amplifiers for conceptual understanding whereby the calculator is used to provide multiple representations of the same situation
3. catalysts for critical thinking by allowing pupils the opportunity to investigate
4. vehicles for integration between different areas of mathematics.

He finishes by saying that 'The graphing calculator is an instrument for student empowerment.'

Graphics calculators for low attaining students

This chapter comes about from a belief that this technology is accessible to pupils of a wider range of attainment and age than is suggested by much of current practice. The *Better Mathematics* report suggests that pupils learn by '. . . experimenting, questioning, reflecting, discovering, investigating and discussing' (Ahmed, 1987, p. 16) and that low attainment can be the result of the restricted and unfulfilling nature of the work given to pupils (p. 14). The use of graphics calculators in the classroom can support teachers in approaching mathematics learning in these ways by offering pupils the opportunity to extend and explore for themselves.

Appropriate use of any technology also allows pupils of all abilities opportunities to work on rich activities. For pupils who find the mechanics of arithmetic difficult, or hard to remember, or who have poor motor skills when graph plotting, for example, a graphics calculator can allow them to extend their thinking further than the limits of their arithmetic or motor skills (see Padfield, 1996, p. 8). Using ICT with low attaining pupils is also important in terms of allowing pupils access to the same facilities as are available to more able pupils in the school. Many low attaining pupils have good spatial skills, and opportunities to build on this allow pupils to develop their mathematical skills more broadly.

Models of classroom use

The activities suggested here build on a number of principles as to the use of graphics calculators in enhancing the teaching and learning of mathematics. Some of the activities use one graphics calculator and a projection device with an overhead projector for mental oral starters or interactive whole-class teaching. This approach allows both for the use of thoughtful, probing questioning for developing concepts in mathematics, and is also a good way for teachers who are less familiar with the technology to make a start on using it in the classroom. Johnston-Wilder, Johnston-Wilder, Pimm and Westwell (1999) report that, 'Some research has shown that if teachers have access to graphic calculators in their lessons, then they tend to ask more high-level questions than they would otherwise do' (p. 155).

In my experience, and that of many other teachers, pupils find graphics calculators easy to use. Many pupils are very familiar with hand-held computer games and other types of technology, and are not overawed by the potential complexity presented by a graphics calculator.

Graphics calculators are also very suitable for running small pieces of software. These can either be written in BASIC and programmed directly in the calculator, or can be written in assembly language and stored in the Flash ROM memory of the calculator. Feedback from recent BECTa projects (see for example, Pope, 2001) suggests that these programs work well in a variety of classroom scenarios – as part of a lesson, used for the whole lesson, and as part of a carousel of activities. Teachers involved in these projects generally found that programs with a competitive element work best, and those programs where pupils were able to have another go if they got the answer wrong had the most impact on pupils' learning.

Some of the activities here use small programs. These can also be an effective way into using the graphics calculator for teachers and pupils because they do not require much knowledge of the workings of the calculator. Many of these small programs are games, which offer children the opportunity to practise skills, develop strategies, investigate, generalise, predict and discuss in mathematics (Padfield, 1996, p. 8).

Ransom and Louch (2000, p. 12) describe a lesson with a group of low attaining Year 7 pupils using graphics calculators. They sum up the positive points from an activity using a small program to practise number bonds to 20 as being:

- quick feedback
- the TI-83 is non-judgemental – you can get it wrong and no one knows but you
- lots of practice
- pace and challenge is there . . .
- you see yourself improve very quickly
- it's a hand-held game machine.

The third use of calculators developed here is that of using the standard functions of a graphics calculator with low attaining pupils.

Sample activities

All the classroom-based work here is based on using the Texas Instruments TI-83 Plus graphics calculator with a viewscreen panel for whole-class display.

1. Using small programs for estimation and rounding

The activities described here focus on developing an understanding of place value and ordering numbers as well as estimation and rounding. These are areas that many low attaining pupils have long-standing difficulty with, as pointed out by Dowker (see

Chapter 3). They are also areas where the graphics calculator may provide an alternative and complementary approach to those used previously. The multi-line display of a graphics calculator also allows pupils to see both the calculation and their answer, and receive feedback on one screen.

In this small program PTLINE, written by Adrian Oldknow, the teacher chooses the start and end points for a number line, which is then displayed on the screen:

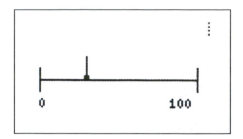

Pupils are then asked to estimate the number the pointer indicates. Pressing ENTER on the calculator reveals the answer:

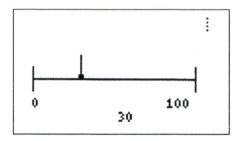

This is an ideal activity for oral and mental work and, either by projecting onto a whiteboard or by using overhead projector film cut to size in the viewscreen window, annotations can be added to show how to divide the line up for estimation.

Classroom questioning might go as follows:

- What number do you think the arrow is pointing to?
- Does anyone think the answer is different?
- How did you decide?
- Can you divide the line up to help you?
- What number is halfway along the line?
- What number is a quarter of the way along the line?
- Are there other ways you could divide up the line?
- Can you mark on any other values?
- How good was your estimate of where the arrow pointed to?

This program can also be used to demonstrate negative number lines:

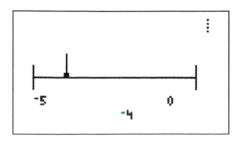

Another small program by Adrian Oldknow called ROUND offers opportunities for both individual and whole-class work on rounding whole numbers to the nearest 10 or 100. Pupils are offered a number and asked to round it. They respond by typing in their answer and the calculator gives them feedback:

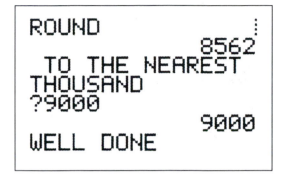
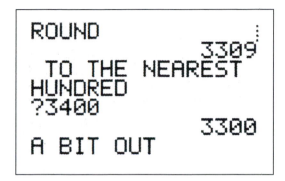

In a whole-class teaching situation, pupils could be asked to respond with their answers and to challenge one another's answers:

- What is eight thousand five hundred and sixty two to the nearest thousand?
- Why?
- Can you draw a diagram to explain why?
- Elaine thinks the answer is eight thousand. Can you explain why she is wrong?
- What number is halfway between eight thousand and nine thousand?

When working individually, pupils could fill in a simple table to provide a record of their work:

Calculator's number	My answer	Right or wrong
8562	9000	▶
3309	3400	▶ 3300

2. Exploring sequences

The multi-line display on a graphics calculator can be used to advantage in using sequences work to count forwards and backwards and to explore number patterns.

The basics of this activity are that a number is entered into the calculator, ENTER is pressed and then an operation is entered. Repeated pressing of ENTER leads to the operation being carried out on the previous term each time:

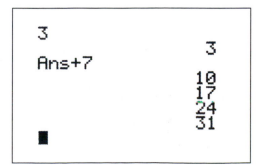

Some of the possibilities for oral and mental work or whole-class teaching by generating sequences in this way are as follows:

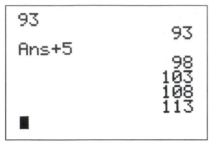

| Counting past 100 | What number comes next?

What patterns can you see?

Will 125 be in this sequence? |

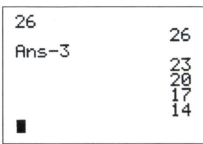

| Counting backwards | What is the next number in the sequence?

What number comes before 26?

Why? |

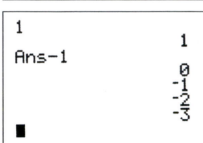

| Counting with negative numbers | What is happening to the numbers?

Which is smaller: –3 or –6?

Can you count backwards in twos? |

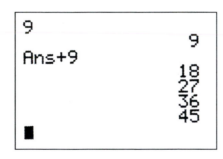

| Exploring number patterns | What patterns can you see in the digits? |

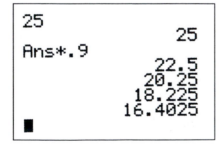

| Multiplying by a decimal between 0 and 1 | Are the numbers getting bigger or smaller?

Can you tell me another sequence where the numbers get smaller each time? |

0.3

Ans+0.3

```
          .3

          .6
          .9
         1.2
         1.5
```

| Adding and subtracting decimals | What is the next number in the sequence?

What does the pattern remind you of?

Is 2.4 in the sequence?

Why? |

One of the advantages of this way of working is that pupils' misconceptions can be explored and erroneous answers can be demonstrated. Any suggestions for sequences given by pupils can easily be generated on the calculator and their properties discussed.

Sequences can also be explored by pupils individually by asking them to make the calculator generate the five times table or to make up a sequence that goes up by 0.2 each time.

These kinds of activity support pupils in developing their basic number work and in consolidating and extending their understanding of the number system. They also allow teachers to focus on areas that typically cause pupils problems, such as counting past 100, counting backwards past zero, the effect of multiplying by a decimal number between 0 and 1 and in working with decimals. Using the graphics calculator allows pupils access to instant feedback, to test conjectures and to explore different sequences and operations quickly and accurately.

Angle estimation program

Many pupils find angle work difficult. They find it difficult to draw and measure angles with a protractor because they have not developed a feel for the size of an angle. Using a small program which displays an angle and asks to enter an estimate for the size of the angle allows pupils to try lots of examples very quickly with instant feedback and, therefore, with the opportunity to improve and develop.

The program used here is an application produced for this calculator by Texas Instruments and is available free of charge from their website (www.education.ti.com). The program allows you to choose the type of angles shown. For each question a diagram is drawn and pupils are asked to input the size of the angle shown. If the size is correct, pupils receive positive feedback. If the answer is incorrect they are shown the question again with a choice of answers to choose from.

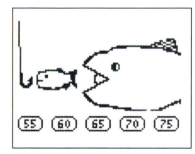

This program is suitable for both whole-class teaching and for pupils working individually or in pairs. In a whole-class situation pupils can be asked to come to a class consensus as to how big the angle is and to explain how they got their answer. Projecting onto a whiteboard, or using overhead projector transparency in the viewscreen window, allows for discussion based on splitting the angle shown into right angles and subdividing further. On an individual basis, the program provides a score at the end and pupils could be asked to record this in their books as feedback on their angle estimation skills.

This activity gives pupils a lot of practice in estimating angles in a short period of time, along with instant feedback and additional support with questions they do incorrectly the first time. It supports pupils in developing a sound basis for angle work by helping them to learn to estimate the size of angles as part of the process of drawing and measuring angles. Because the images in the graphics calculator program are dynamic, pupils also have angle as a measure of turn reinforced.

Supporting teachers in developing graphics calculator use

All the examples in this chapter have been used with teachers and trainee teachers in helping them to make more effective use of graphics calculators in their teaching and with their pupils. They provide a small snapshot of a few of the possibilities in using graphics calculators to support the learning of low attaining students in mathematics.

In developing work using graphics calculators with their classes there are a number of things teachers need to consider. In common with using many forms of ICT there are issues relating to the recording of pupils' work. This is an issue teachers need to consider when planning lessons. In many cases it is appropriate for pupils not to write down all that they have done, and for those pupils who find writing difficult this may be a positive experience for them, allowing them to achieve more than they would otherwise. However, pupils could be asked to make some sketches, to write down some reflection on their learning at the end of the lesson or to record their score of a game, for example. Alternatively, if a computer and printer with the appropriate connection lead and Graphlink or TI Connect software are available, pupils could print out their graphics calculator screen as a record of their work.

Teachers also need to give consideration to managing resources. Many departments using graphics calculators have in-house procedures to ensure that the calculators are either reset at the end of a previous lesson or at the beginning of the next. Such systems mean that there are fewer problems at the start of the lesson, where pupils can become frustrated because the calculator isn't set up correctly or because their graph is overlaid with someone else's work. A simple storage rack will allow the calculators to be counted out and checked in at the beginning and end of lessons to minimise loss of and damage to equipment.

Use of whole-screen display is always beneficial as it allows the teacher to check that pupils have the correct screen displayed and in order to work with the whole class. It is often very effective for pupils to work in pairs using graphics calculators as they can then support each other as well as being a means of promoting mathematical discussion. Teachers should also consider whether pupils need to be provided with a printed instruction sheet to support their work. Posters are also available for teachers to use to indicate the location of the buttons on the calculator.

The internet is a very rich source of support, materials and ideas for using graphics calculators in the teaching of mathematics. There are also a number of organisations, such as T[3] (Teachers Teaching with Technology, www.t3.org), that offer training to teachers in using graphics calculators. The BECTa website contains links to such resources (http://www.becta.org.uk/technology/infosheets/html/graphcalc.html) for all the major manufacturers of graphics calculators. Journals such as *Micromath* also offer lots of support and ideas for using graphics calculators and other technology, as does Oldknow and Taylor's (2000) book.

Teachers do not need to write small programs themselves unless they wish to, as there are many high quality programs available on the internet for downloading, both from Texas Instruments (www.education.ti.com) and other sites such as www.madmaths.net.

Conclusions

Graphics calculators have a recognised place in the use of ICT in the teaching of mathematics. They are accessible to, and their use is beneficial to, pupils of all ages and levels of attainment. They offer benefits in terms of flexibility and accessibility in that they are easy to use and can be used by pupils as part of their ordinary mathematics lessons.

References

AHMED, A. (Project Director) (1987) *Better Mathematics*. LAMP Report. London: HMSO.

BARBOUR, R. and BETHEL, F. (1995) We have seen the future, and its screen is small . . . *Mathematics in School*, 24(4), 20–1.

BECTA (1999) *Curriculum Software Initiative: Mathematics*. Online at http://www.becta.org.uk/technology/software/curriculum/reports/maths.html

BECTA (2000) *Mathematics – A Pupil's Entitlement*. Online at vtc.ngfl.gov.uk/uploads/text/secondary-17805.pdf

BECTA (2001) *Information Sheet on Graphical Calculators*. Online at http://www.becta.org.uk/technology/infosheets/pdf/graphcalc.pdf

DfEE (2001) *Framework for Teaching Mathematics: Years 7, 8 and 9*. London: DfEE.

JOHNSTON-WILDER, S., JOHNSTON-WILDER, P., PIMM, D. and WESTWELL, J. (eds) (1999) *Learning to Teach Mathematics in the Secondary School*. London: Routledge.

OLDKNOW, A. and TAYLOR, R. (2000) *Teaching Mathematics with ICT*. London: Continuum.

PADFIELD, E. (1996) Developing an investigational approach to the teaching and learning of mathematics. *Equals*, 2(1), 8–11.

POPE, S. (2001) *Hand Held Technology Report*. Online at http://vtc.ngfl.gov.uk/uploads/application/Suefinalreport-60825.doc

RANSOM, P. and LOUCH, H. (2000) Who says calculators don't improve numeracy? *Mathematics in School*, 29(2), 11–13.

RUTHVEN, K. (1994) Supercalculators and the secondary mathematics curriculum. In M. Selinger, *Teaching Mathematics*, 154–68. London: Routledge.

SMITH, J. P. (1998, updated 2002) *Graphing Calculators in the Mathematics Classroom*. ERIC Digest. Online at http://www.ericse/org/digests/dse98-4.html

CHAPTER 11

Generalising arithmetic: an alternative to algebra (or things to do with a plastic bag)

STEPHANIE PRESTAGE and PAT PERKS

The fortnight after the half term of the autumn term 2001, the second year of the new century, saw an interesting Orwellian phenomenon. We had each responded to cries for help from Crewe to London, from friends and family with Year 7 sons and daughters. The cause of the problem was algebra – seemingly being covered by Year 7 pupils throughout the land. We checked the planning sheets provided by the National Numeracy Strategy (NNS) Key Stage 3 *Framework for Teaching Mathematics* (DfEE, 2001) and, indeed, found algebra prescribed for the second half of the autumn term. Our brief survey revealed that many of the Year 7s had no notion of what this 'algebra' stuff is all about. 'What is two more than x?' we asked. Resoundingly, the favourite answer was z.

The NNS has a policy of equal opportunity. All students in each school year are given the opportunity to learn the same mathematics. In this chapter, we will consider the role of the NNS algebra curriculum for KS3 students and, particularly, for low attaining students in mathematics for whom alternatives are vital in maintaining an interesting curriculum diet. In particular, we will present a rethink on algebra as a complementary way of working on and with arithmetic, as a way of generalising about arithmetic. The *Framework for Teaching Mathematics* does talk about generalised arithmetic and, in fact, the opening sentence to the section introducing algebra confirms that: 'Algebra in Key Stage 3 is generalised arithmetic' (DfEE, 2001, p. 14). However, we would like to replace the noun *generalised* with the verb *generalising* and reveal the possibilities offered within the activity of *generalising arithmetic* rather than the teaching of algebra. Working with algebra for generalising arithmetic can help all students to develop their numeracy skills and capabilities with number. Working algebraically in this way can provide a grown-up environment for practising the four rules, without offering low attaining students their practice as pages of mind-numbing sums. We advocate a change to the order of the algebra curriculum and have used this approach successfully in classrooms with a range of students from Year 5 to Year 9. In fact, this article is not about teaching mathematics differently to students with special educational needs, but is about considering better ways to teach some mathematics for all students.

Algebra in the *Framework*

The Framework sections the Year 7 algebra curriculum under the two headings, *Equations, formulae and identities* and *Sequences, functions and graphs*. Under these headings are three statements in bold – the key algebra objectives for Year 7:

- Use letter symbols to represent unknown numbers and variables.
- Understand that algebraic operations follow the same conventions and order as arithmetic operations.
- Plot the graphs of simple linear functions.

We will be working on these three key objectives throughout this chapter in the activities and ideas we present. The remaining statements of the teaching programme are given as a list in the Framework document (DfEE, 2001, section 3, p. 6). Ignore the implied hierarchy of the list. If you work on the three key objectives you will subsume most of the remaining ideas in the algebra curriculum for Year 7s (and beyond): things such as collecting like terms, constructing and solving simple linear equations, generating and describing simple linear sequences given a rule. In fact, by the end of this chapter we will have mentioned most of the algebra in the GCSE intermediate syllabus.

Some thoughts about teaching and learning

Advice in the Framework is highly specific. In the autumn term of Year 7 you are advised to spend six hours on sequences and functions and, later, five hours on equations. In the spring term there are six hours on these plus integers, powers and roots, followed later by four hours on all three. In the summer term these three areas are revisited for eight hours. The recipe of the three-part lesson and the seeming prescription of the order of content and time spent can create immense pedagogical conflict for those working with low achieving students. And so we offer some of our beliefs about teaching and learning – apologies if all of this seems obvious.

The sectionalising of the Framework and the suggested timings, plus the issue of working at level 5, playing catch-up and the other implications for Year 7, undervalue the importance of matching teaching and the pace of learning. The content for Year 7 offers pupils an opportunity to work mathematically, but achieving understanding depends on the teacher offering the necessary space for learning. All learners need to work in an environment where they are valued and seen to be working mathematically. They need time and space in which to think, share and discuss what their ideas are. They must not be ridiculed by a system which only values the one correct 'right' answer, but ought to enjoy the many possibilities which allow them to develop. Working with algebra *can* offer an environment to do this.

School students are often very trusting, but they can be helped in their learning by creating a 'need to know'. Faced with an equation such as $2x + 3 = 17$, most learners have no experience of why such learning might be of value (for many it is not; it more often just provides a way of testing number). By this we don't necessarily mean creating a reality but creating a purpose and perhaps capturing the imagination using the type of curiosity which makes people do puzzles of many types.

Five issues

Before we explore the transformation of the teaching of algebra into working on the generalising of arithmetic, we outline some of the issues that obstruct the learning of algebra.

A first issue – remembering number bonds

One of the more unfortunate aspects of being a low achiever in mathematics is the often over-indulgence in a diet of simple sums: never simple to those having to do them, and frustrating for teachers who are trying to take students through the demands of the Framework. If you do not understand how arithmetic generalises, it becomes difficult to see patterns. If you cannot see patterns, each sum is unrelated to any other you have done. For example, the sum $7 + 3 = 10$ is seen to be different from $3 + 7 = 10$. Similarly, you might know your three times table and remember $7 \times 3 = 21$ but are not comfortable with the seven times table and so cannot easily give the answer to 3×7. Remembering number bonds is a major mountain to climb, because there are no patterns to help. Knowing that addition and multiplication are commutative (order does not matter) are powerful generalisations.

A second issue – meaning of operations, or, the Alice dilemma

A big hurdle when working with algebraic expressions is their lack of closure. Expressions in arithmetic can be worked out; for example, sums like $3 + 4$, $35 \div 7$ reduce to one number, because the operator tells you what to do. $3 + 4$ is 7, because $3 + 4 = 7$; if you add four more to three you obtain seven. $3 + 4$ is not seen as a single number, it is a combination of numbers under the operation of addition, which you can do. So the pupil sees an operation and responds knowing this means 'Do something'. The equals sign also requires a response as the pupils are taught from an early age to read mathematics from left to right, sums like $3 + 4 =$ are presented as things to be completed, the = sign tends to mean complete the sum.

In algebra the mathematical world is presented differently, $x + 3$ is a number, there is nothing to do, the operation of addition is not an indication to do something. Similarly $x + 3 = 10$ refers to the equality of two things, the $x + 3$ with the 10; the + sign is not an indication to do something; the = sign is also not an indication to do something. The mathematical worlds of arithmetic and of algebra are different worlds to inhabit when reading signs. If pupils stay in their first world of arithmetic, reading the signs and symbols in the algebraic world becomes problematic. Like Alice when she went through the looking glass, things are not as they seem, and the consequences of applying the logic of the arithmetic world to the algebra world can be mathematically disastrous. For example, if you stay in the arithmetic world the expression $x + 2$ must equal something because the addition sign says 'Do something', so why not z? Very logical. A more complicated expression like $2x - 17$ holds an enormous amount of information for the mathematician, the equation $2x - 17 = 3x + 23$ offers even more. These expressions and equations are presented as compressed pieces of information, in current ICT parlance the files have been 'zipped'. This is very useful if these are to be used in conjunction with other things, but too dense if, as is the case with our learners, you not only have to solve equations but first of all come to read them and to understand them.

A third issue – working with codes

One of the textbook approaches to algebra is to use codes. Such approaches can be found in a variety of guises, all of which use the arithmetical world for sign reading.

Consider the following textbook activity:

> If a = 1, b = 2, c = 3, d = 4 and so on, decode
> a + b, d − a, a × b, d + c, c × (a + b)

This particular example provides arithmetic practice with reward, but the reference to a = 1, b = 2 etc. reinforces the use of constants and encourages an inappropriate sense of algebra by assuming a + 1 = b and $x + 2 = z$. Here is a second familiar example.

> Let   x = 2   y = 3
> Complete the following   x + y =

The sign reading here is mainly in the arithmetic world. The 'add' sign means add the two numbers together and the 'equals' sign means place the result on the other side. Starting with codes makes the reading of algebraic expressions even more obscure and acts to reinforce the idea of the possibility of closure in an algebraic expression.

A fourth issue – fruit salad algebra

Fruit salad is another popular starting point for working with substitution. Much has been written about the nonsense problems with fruit salad algebra, problems such as 'I have three apples and four bananas so the total cost is 3a + 4b', but is that three apples and four bananas? And where does money come in? Or 'I have three apples and four bananas so a + b = 7' but is that seven pieces of fruit? Is it any wonder that children are confused? This confusion can be made worse by examples such as one seen the other day: the symbol for metres and the variable m are interchanged.

> If the length of the trailer is t and the length of the car is c and their total length is 11m then t + c = 11m

A fifth issue – starting with 'simple' linear equations

The early advice in the Framework is to build on the experience of manipulating number equations like 8 × 6 = 48 and all its variations in order to extend to the manipulation of equations such as ab = c (DfEE, p. 14). Having worked with number equations, the advice for teaching the section on *Equations, formulae and identities* continues:

> The initial approach to manipulating number statements needs to extend into a set of rules for solving equations under a general heading 'Do the same to both sides of the equation'.
>
> (DfEE, p. 15)

Essentially the pupil task here is to work on solving equations, to find the unknown – a starting point also often made by text books. The task is 'simple' and code-like, and there is only one answer! But the task has very little to do with generalisation. In most cases the solution depends on knowing number bonds, as in: 'solve', or even those earlier box-type questions: ' □ + □ = 10'. The presence of the x in the equation offers another hurdle but is a complete irrelevance and makes the problem look complicated. In fact, if you know your number bonds there is no problem to solve, something plus seven equals ten, must mean that the something is three, no rules are needed. Additionally there is no generality, only a specific case.

Our Orwellian experience last November occurred because many students are expected to practise the algorithm for solving linear equations before they even know what an expression is. The over-attention in the Framework to the equals sign (cf. DfEE, p. 14) gives the impression that it is only the formal expression of equations which is valued. Many pupils need firstly to appreciate the idea of an expression containing a letter, to understand the idea of a variable which lies at the heart of algebra. This does not mean that we do not believe that the idea of equality should not be worked on, but there are many ways of doing this informally. By the way, it also seems to us inappropriate that the Framework should recommend the algorithm 'Do the same to both sides of the equation'. We prefer the doing and undoing notion for solving equations with the use of inverse operations – though no doubt you have your own preference.

Working with variables: ban the equals sign

Knowing that 3 more than x is $x + 3$, and that $x + 3$ is itself a number are powerful concepts and essential for working in this area of mathematics. Knowing that although $x + 3$ is dependent upon the value of x, mathematicians can work with this expression without needing to know the value of x, is also a powerful piece of knowledge. Therefore, we suggest that you work with your students with variables. Essentially, ban the equals sign! Work on expressions, and as a consequence work (as we will show) on activities that are about generalising arithmetic. Remember, when you work on tasks such as 'I am two more than s and you are three more than me, how much more are you than s?' you are working on number bonds explicitly and the language of comparison. Don't formalise the mathematics too early. Some classes may only need an hour, others may need two weeks, but the idea of a variable and an expression must be understood by all before it is worth going any further. Our experience tells us that some bright Year 5 pupils absorbed the formality after about a week and a so-called 'bottom set' Year 9 group was still working at the informal level after a fortnight. Some groups may need a long time to work with expressions, but as they work with them they are practising lots of arithmetic.

We now return to the three key algebra objectives from the Framework (listed on page 116). There is no doubt that these are vital to learning how to manipulate and solve algebraic expressions and equations that make up the remaining curriculum detail. The splurge diagram (Figure 1) shows the other aspects of mathematics that we will be working on.

A possible teaching sequence and some activities

Any suggested teaching sequence or activity needs interpretation and so these ideas are given with a health warning. You will have to place these ideas within your own school, departmental and classroom context and time constraints. The main aspects of mathematics described here focus on creating and using expressions leading, consequently, to working intuitively on many aspects of mathematical structure.

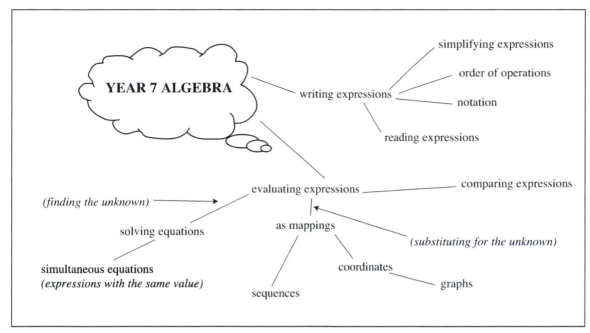

Figure 1. Splurge of algebra

Creating expressions

In fact, these ideas all started with an empty plastic bag and a group of Year 5 pupils. Here is an extract from the lesson notes describing the first lesson on algebra.

We took an empty plastic bag into the classroom. I started the lesson as we had planned and said, 'This bag is not in fact empty. I have x things in this bag [some miming] and I will put two more into the bag [more mime]. I now have x + 2 things in this bag. [Pause] Does anyone else want to join in?' [The pupils looked nervous] Shirley, the class teacher, took up the cause with her story: 'I have s things in this bag and I will remove four of them [lots of mime]. I now have s – 4 things in this bag.' After a couple more exchanges between us with the bag, a pupil, Tom, asked if he could have a go. With a large grin on his face, he offered his own drama and a completely correct expression t + 20. More became brave and joined in. Amazingly, after not very long, along with expressions like the ones we had given (variations on the theme with addition and subtraction) we also had variables added to variables such as s + t, as well as the beginnings of multiplication such as a + a, a + a + a and double t and then one of them wanted to do some squaring!! The energy in the room was tangible. When nearly everyone was offering ideas, the expressions were written on the board and we went on to work with these in an activity. We were ready to collect like terms and use the notation 2x for equivalence to x + x. And then we nudged with more terms in the expression. The reading of expressions became woven with the creation of expressions.

The actual dynamics of the lesson cannot be recreated – which just proves how hard it is to convey education material at a distance – but this group of nine-year-olds was content to use their imagination to do some mathematics. Imagination, not reality, was the vital ingredient to creating these expressions. In the third lesson we used a box of *Multilink* to repeat the ideas (too many things to count) and added and removed some, which also worked well. Recently these ideas were used with a group of Year 7s, for whom even the bag was imaginary by the third lesson. When you need some expressions to work with for a lesson, you might create them anew each time. It is important to move beyond specific cases, to let the students know that the activities that follow can be worked on with any expressions. You have to build in, in some way, the generality of the situation.

Working with expressions

Once the class is comfortable with creating expressions, create a few flashcards to work on ordering of expressions. Sheets of A4 paper would do in the first instance as you trial these ideas. Choose a different letter every time you work on this. Once you have a sense of the activities, you can create different routes to suit your purpose.

Activity a
Get two students to the front and give them cards to hold up. (Alternatively they can have their own cards, or pairs might work together.)

Cards (e.g.): $\boxed{x}$ $\boxed{x + 2}$

Give x a value, and ask the rest of the class to chant the value for the other pupil. Ask for different values of x, with more chanting. (Change the cards for more practice.)

Possible mathematics
Implicit working on idea of dependent and independent variables, substitution.

Having begun the idea of variables and substitution, the pupils are ready to work on some arithmetic ideas.

Activity b
Get three students to the front and give them cards to hold up.

Cards (e.g.): $\boxed{x}$ $\boxed{x + 2}$ $\boxed{x + 5}$

Give x a value, ask them to stand in order. Ask for different values of x, ask them to stand in order. Is there a value of x that changes the order?

Possible mathematics
Implicit ordering of 0, 2 and 5.

Generalising to ordering numbers such as 20, 22, 25 or 7, 9 and 12; generalising adding odd and even numbers.

Implicit working on idea of dependent and independent variables, substitution.

The main teaching point here is that the repetition of ideas creates the opportunity for generalising about the arithmetic. While you are working on ordering you will need to work with substitution. It is substitution that allows the arithmetic practice and offers a generality about odd and even numbers, or ideas about adding 2 and adding 5. Working on $x + 2$ for lots of values of x and comparing the results with what happens with $x + 5$, say, offers an alternative insight into the structure behind the arithmetic to a set of sums, even when a conscious design feature is to look at the relationship in the repeated operation. Students tend to see each question as separate, not looking for a link.

What about odds and evens?

Activity c

| x | | $x + 2$ | | $x + 5$ |

Choose one of the cards and ask, if this is odd, what about the others?

Choose a card and ask, if this ends in 2, what do the others end in?

If $x + 2$ is in the three times table, which others are? (A large multiplication grid would be a useful resource here.) If $8 - x$ is in the four times table, what about any of the other cards?

Mathematics

Odds, evens, three times tables.

From here on, the rest of the ideas in this section are variations on the theme (see Prestage and Perks, 2001). Add in more cards, change the number set, extend the expressions. The time that you offer for an activity depends entirely on you – ten minutes to a week. Oh, and don't be afraid of repetition; repetition creates a comfort zone for the students. Also, repetition offers the arithmetic practice as the algebraic expressions of a structure on which to hang the remembering of those number bonds.

Activity d

Add extra cards and students:

such as . . . | $x + 12$ | | $x + 3$ |

or | $x - 4$ | | $x + 7$ | | $x - 1$ |

or | $x - 3$ | | $x + 20$ | | $x + 10$ |

Possible mathematics

Implicit ordering of 12 and 3 in relation to 0, 2 and 5.

Generalising to ordering numbers such as 32 and 23 with 20, 22, 25.

Depending on what you include, more about ordering and substitution.

Once you are happy with students developing a sense of ordering and expressions as numbers, add some more ambiguity. Work on inequality as well as equality, the former offering lots of practice at doing arithmetic.

Activity e
Add extra cards and students:

$$\boxed{x + x} \quad \boxed{5 - x}$$

Can $5 - x$ be slotted in? Is there ambiguity – do we need to check values?

Start working on inequality by questions such as, when is $x + x$ smaller than $x + 5$?

Possible mathematics
Reading expressions, notation, set of solutions to the inequality questions.

Then move to introduce coefficients (our experience is that these expressions need repeated explanation and not formal teaching) and then use the coefficients to build new expressions so that $2x + 1$ is easily 'read' as 'double x add one' and $3x - 4$ is 'read' as three times x subtract four. What about powers? Again don't make this extra aspect 'difficult' by over-teaching – explain the notation and stay with powers and numbers that they can solve mentally (or give them a calculator to resolve disputes) – stay with the mathematics for your group. Remember that square numbers are one of the important structures of the multiplication tables!

Activity f
Add extra cards and students:

$$\boxed{2x} \quad \boxed{3x} \quad \boxed{x^2}$$

How is $2x$ related to $x + x$? Do you need the card 'Double x' as well?

Possible mathematics
Formal notation for coefficients, reading expressions, collecting like terms, relation between this mapping and the two times tables.

Can we stress again that we suggest lots of repetition, building towards a comfort zone before adding on the next layers of difficulty. At any point you might start back at the beginning, working with decimals or fractions as the value for x. These ideas then become useful starters ... or middles ... or ends! What you want is to offer many opportunities to work on the ideas. Add other cards or make a different set for another day.

If you wanted to work on the three times table, you may wish to work with cards such as:

$$x + x + x \qquad 3x \qquad 2x + x \qquad 4x - x \qquad 8x - 5x$$

You may then find students offering ideas such as $x + x - x + 2x + 7x - x - 5x - x$ or even $99x \div 33$. This will also be the moment for giggles as students begin to realise there are lots of answers and they can find them. They are collecting like terms without any explanations to confuse and they are working on finding formats for three.

What would happen if you were to add another variable? Suppose you had sets of cards such as:

x	y	$x + y$	$x - y$	$8 - x$
$8 - y$	$2x + 7$	$2y + 7$	$2x - 5$	$2y + 1$

How might you order these? Where are any the same? How might you explain these? What if you were to work with these cards?

a	a + b	a + 2b	a + 3b	a + 4b etc.

What happens if you were to add:

a – b	a – 2b	a – 3b	a – 4b etc.

The variations are endless, and that is only with the cards as flashcards. The above activities have been described in terms of whole-class participation and people as the major resource. They are easily adapted to small-group work, by using small cards where the group has to make decisions with which all agree. The cards can be ordered or sorted. Sorting into pairs (or more) which are always the same, sometimes the same or never the same is a wonderful way of forcing more practice. The explanations also allow students to gain greater insight into arithmetic structure.

Here is a summary activity.

Summary activity
Work with ten cards and students

x	$3x$	$2x$	$2x - 5$	$8 - x$

$3x + 1$	$9 - x$	$2x + 3$	$2x - 3$	$-x$

Ask the student holding x to declare his or her value. (There are lots of ways you can vary the language of equality here – 'What is the value of x?', 'What is x equal to?', 'What is x worth?') Another value of x is then declared.

The rest of the students have to shuffle themselves into the order of the value of their cards. Alternatively, this could be done with each student having his or her own set of cards and someone declares a value for x.

Nowhere does the problem have to be formalised – it is not necessary to write: 'If $x = 3$ what is the value of $2x + 3$?' Although you could if you feel the students are ready for such formality. The time and place for formalisation is a teaching decision based on the learners' understanding and needs. For many pupils, working with the arithmetic in this different form is sufficient. The multiple opportunities for practice and challenge are enough for useful mathematical development. The many different answers as you subtract a value for x and subtract from 8 can give more insight into the structure of arithmetic than the separate sums.

And so to some extensions; building on the same ideas, here are some thoughts about inequalities, simultaneous equations and solving equations based on the summary activity. All are mainly intuitive, there are no algorithms to follow, no rules. The students are working on the mathematics and not having to spend all their energy on remembering what to do. In fact, any one of these activities might be used as an extension at any stage of algebra teaching – none of them are to be seen as 'hard' extensions to earlier activities. Please don't think that the linear sequence of our writing implies any hierarchy. Make your own choices.

Inequalities

What if x chooses another value, who has to move? Why?

Will some students always be together? This offers lots of opportunity for practice and discussion.

$2x$ $2x - 5$ $2x + 3$ $2x - 3$ can be ordered consistently, but where do the others fit?

Could any of the cards fit between $2x - 5$ and $2x - 3$?

(We are now on higher level GCSE mathematics, but the intuition about arithmetic and the practice could help us stumble on such ideas without forcing anyone to go down that road. We could make up a really nasty question, which formalised would frighten your most gifted KS3 mathematician,

for what values of x is $2x - 5 < x < 2x - 3$,

and yet you could find one solution by accident, playing the above.)

Simultaneous equations

And so it is possible to get into work with simultaneous equations. For some values of x more than one student may be the same number, why?

This can be easy to explain, but formalised as:

$2x + 3 = 3x + 1$ when $x = 2$

It looks threatening and makes no sense to many learners.

> **Solving equations**
> Ask $9 - x$ for his/her value, the others have to order themselves.
>
> At this point the possibilities are endless. Any one of the cards might declare his/her value and so the pupils are solving many equations.

Formally we would then be working on:

$$9 - x = 13 \rightarrow x = -4 \text{ or } 9 - x = 13 \rightarrow 2x - 3 = -11$$

But for most Year 7 you would not mention this, unless they got interested in this condensed notation. Or you could link back to it if you ever wanted to work on simultaneous equations. What if the student with the card $3x + 1$ chose the number 8? Do we need to work with exact numbers, or could x be 2 and a bit? How do we work out the other numbers? What levels of accuracy might you work to?

> **Sequences and graphs**
> Get two students to the front and give them cards to hold up.
>
> Cards (e.g.): $\boxed{x}$ $\boxed{x + 2}$
>
> Give x a value, ask the rest of the class to chant the value of $x + 2$. Give different values of x, ask for more chanting. On the board write the mapping $x \rightarrow x + 2$ and put the numbers down as they are created. Create coordinate pairs from these mappings and plot the points.
>
> Change the mapping.

Conclusion

All of the activities we have offered are based on an assumption of the need for everyone to practise arithmetic regularly and that algebra has always offered our higher attaining students the opportunity to rehearse their number bonds in a 'grown-up' context. It can also be so for those achieving at lower levels as well who are just as deserving of a grown-up approach. The learning of number bonds also needs an algebraic framework to scaffold learners' understanding to aid memory. Working with the expressions x and $x + 3$ offers a framework for adding three and subtracting three, by starting with the generalised arithmetic and using specialising to create an understanding of generalising. Also, by working on algebra as generalising arithmetic, we reduce the frustration of the 'It's too hard' to the acceptable challenge of 'That's easy'.

References

DfEE (2001) *Key Stage 3 National Strategy, Framework for Teaching Mathematics: Years 7, 8 and 9.* London: DfEE Publications.

PRESTAGE, S. and PERKS, P. (2001) *Adapting and Extending Secondary Mathematics: New tasks for old*. London: David Fulton Publishers.

Looking forward

All the chapters in this book contain, explicitly or implicitly, guidance for future practice which might lead to improving mathematics teaching and learning for those who might otherwise fail to learn. In the current climate such students are often taught in ways which conform to a 'delivery' metaphor of knowledge. Frequent testing, combined with a fragmentary approach to the curriculum and a well-intentioned emphasis on 'basic skills', leads to a repetitive curriculum for such students. This may serve to consolidate failure rather than enhance their abilities to act mathematically in the world by developing existing proficiencies.

In the final section we have drawn together three chapters about the main perspectives of the book: support, thinking and inclusion. By placing these last we want to show that a different climate for mathematical achievement is possible for all students. We want to move away from the 'treatment' metaphor for students who are not managing to learn mathematics and think instead about including all in the full mathematics curriculum by developing the intellectual and mental tools for taking part, and for proficient, positive, knowledgeable support.

CHAPTER 12

Watching, listening and acting: a case study of learning support assistants in primary mathematics lessons

JENNY HOUSSART

Introduction

In this chapter I consider the issue of what action LSAs might take as a result of what they see and hear. It arises from my participant observation research in primary mathematics lessons with low attaining students, in which I assumed a role similar to that of the LSAs who also worked in the classrooms. During my first year of research with a Year 5 set, I noticed just how much LSAs are able to see and hear. In my writing at the time I talked about the importance of some use being made of what the LSA saw, for example by feeding information back to the teacher (Houssart, 2001, see Chapter 5). When my work extended to other classes, I realised that there were differences in practice in how the LSAs I worked alongside reacted when they noticed something about the children they were working near. This chapter explores possible approaches, with emphasis on a case study of successful practice. It goes on to consider the impact of different approaches on the children's learning of mathematics.

Background

The role of LSAs

As Balshaw (1999) demonstrates, there has been an increase in the use of assistants in schools, accompanied by changes in their role and the way they are viewed. In particular, she suggests that where practice is effective, they are seen as partners in the classroom rather than merely helpers. However, recent research suggests that there is a wide range of practice as far as the role of assistants is concerned (Farrell, Balshaw and Polat, 1999). This is confirmed by Tennant (2001), writing about support in the context of mathematics lessons. He suggests that the provision of extra adults in a classroom may not enhance the learning of children and gives examples in which he felt there was no effective communication between LSAs and teachers and no evidence of building effective teamwork. However, he also acknowledges that he has had contact with LSAs who have more positive experiences and feel their judgements are valued and taken into account.

In discussing inclusive mathematics in primary schools, Robbins (2000) considers the role of support staff and acknowledges possible difficulties. One point he makes is that LSAs can be frustrated by the unwillingness of teachers to utilise their talents and abilities. He also says that there can be confusion about the role of assistants – a confusion which can be shared by the teacher, the assistant and the children.

Teamwork

In defining effective practice, Farrell et al. (1999) make a number of points about communication and teamwork between teachers and assistants. For example, they say that teachers who recognise the potential of gaining feedback are better able to capitalise on LSA perspectives. They go on to suggest that immediate verbal feedback is most effective. Their recommendations for effective practice include the suggestions that LSAs work cooperatively with teachers and contribute to lesson evaluation.

However, the literature does acknowledge that working as a team is a complex issue. Balshaw (1999) acknowledges the complexity of the role of assistant and the tensions associated with it. In seeking to assist schools in developing policy and practice she offers six principles. One of these principles is that LSAs should be valued members of a working team. The other principles concern clarity of roles, communication, consistency of approach, use of skills and staff development needs. In expanding on the idea of a working team, she says that assistants should be valued for their contribution to the team in ways that are made explicit, thus creating a climate of respect among the adults.

The difficulty and complexity of classroom teamwork is acknowledged by Thomas (1992), whose research considers the impact of extra adults in the classroom, including parents, support teachers and ancillary helpers. He suggests that the demise of team-teaching is evidence of the problems of teamwork. In discussing potential problems in more detail, the issues considered include the importance of role definition and the apparently marginal position of extra adults in the classroom. One situation in which he suggests some extra adults feel they can be of little use is when the teacher is talking to the whole class. This point is made by support teachers he interviews and reinforced by his own experience as a support teacher.

The LSA role during direct teaching

The issue of whether extra adults can be of use when the teacher is talking to the whole class is relevant to the use of LSAs in the implementation of the Numeracy Strategy, an initiative just introduced into English primary schools when this research was carried out. Within the strategy, there is a focus on direct teaching as well as a suggestion that each lesson should start with whole-class oral and mental work. One of the main documents connected with the strategy, the *Framework for Teaching Mathematics* (DfEE, 1999), talks specifically, though briefly, about the role of support staff during whole-class oral work. It says they should position themselves close to children who need special help and provide it discreetly. In addition, it says that they should observe carefully the responses of the children they will be working with later in the lesson, to inform the support they will give.

There seems to be some agreement that LSAs are likely to hear and see things of importance. For example, in a handbook for classroom assistants (Aplin, 1998), a section is devoted to the importance of listening to children. In the short part of the book addressed to teachers, there is also discussion of the assistant's role at the beginning and ending of a mathematics lesson. It is suggested that a valuable use of the assistant is to focus on particular children and monitor their response.

The listening and watching part of the LSA's role seems to be reasonably well established. 'What next?' seems to be more open to question. One possible dilemma is whether assistants can say anything straight away as a result of what they notice. This relates to the question of whether they should say anything at all when the teacher is addressing the class. A related issue is whether any such remarks should be addressed to the teacher, to individual children, or to the class as a whole. Fox (1998) considers that this is one of the things that should be discussed when assistants and teachers establish the ground rules for working together. She suggests eight questions that assistants could ask the teacher they work with as part of this process. One of these questions is 'Can I contribute or ask questions during the lesson?' (p. 10). A variant of this question is considered in more detail here. My version is about what interventions are possible and appropriate as a result of what LSAs see or hear in a mathematics lesson. This will be considered in the next section by exploring some possible scenarios.

Possible scenarios

The following scenarios are suggested in order to prompt questions about what an LSA might do in particular situations. They are suggested here because they relate to the case study that follows, though they may also form a useful starting point for discussions between groups of teachers and LSAs.

Suppose the LSA feels that one of the following is happening:

- a particular child is struggling with the work being explained by the teacher
- a particular activity is not working too well for several children
- the work is too easy for one or several of the children
- the teacher is saying something which is confusing, or even incorrect
- the amount of time allowed for a task is inappropriate for some children.

How might the LSA react in these situations? Some possibilities are:

- do nothing, say nothing
- raise the issue with the teacher tactfully, after the lesson
- raise the issue openly when it occurs and in the hearing of the children
- take action to deal with the issue without consulting the teacher.

The scenarios suggested may provoke different reactions from teachers. Reactions may range from feeling these things only happen in 'bad' classrooms, through an acknowledgement that they can sometimes happen to most of us, to the view that they represent the complexities of teaching and learning and are ever present. Another key issue is that all the scenarios hinge on the LSA's opinion of what is happening. How seriously they are taken will depend on how highly the view of the LSA is valued, especially if it potentially contradicts that of the teacher. One approach is that teachers are highly trained experts, so their view is paramount. Certainly the training and knowledge of the LSA is a closely related issue, and this varies widely. However, there are other points to consider. One is that LSAs are in an excellent position to observe and listen to individual children, partly because they do not normally have the teacher's role of maintaining an awareness of the whole room, delivering the lesson and considering what changes to make. Another point is that some LSAs work closely with individual children, sometimes across several years, and build up a picture of strengths and difficulties that a teacher might not have, especially in the context of 'setting', where the maths teacher may only teach the child for one hour a day.

My experience of working alongside teachers and LSAs in 'bottom' mathematics sets, containing a high proportion of children with special needs, is that very different approaches can be taken from the scenarios listed above. In one classroom, for example, LSAs often took no action in such situations, though they occasionally shared their observations quietly with each other. The view seemed to be that other adults were not expected to speak when the teacher was teaching the class. There was also a feeling that making suggestions or pointing out problems, even tactfully and outside the hearing of children, was an unacceptable threat to the teacher's authority. In another classroom, however, I noticed that LSAs would commonly raise issues with the teacher as they occurred. They would also sometimes discuss issues afterwards, or occasionally take action themselves. This latter classroom is considered as a case study in the following section. I have selected incidents to match some of the scenarios listed above. The main issue in my mind when considering the incidents is what possible impact they had on the children's learning of mathematics.

Case study

Context

This work was carried out with a small 'bottom' maths set in a large primary school. The children were mixed Year 3 and Year 4. All were considered to have special needs as far as mathematics is concerned, and some had statements. The teacher, Mrs Baxter, was supported by two LSAs, Mrs Taylor and Mrs Carrington. The latter was assigned to work mainly with one child, James. In the classroom all three adults were normally adressed using 'Mrs' and their surname. In the descriptions which follow, I will refer to the two LSAs in this way, in order to distinguish them clearly from the children and the teacher.

I was present at lessons once a week as part of my research into mathematical tasks. While researching I took on a role similar to that of the two LSAs, working alongside children as directed by the teacher. When possible, I made notes about the responses of children to mathematical tasks. I was often able to do that when the teacher was teaching the whole class. The following incidents were all recorded in my field notes. They were recorded originally because of my interest in the child's response to a mathematical task. They are chosen to be reproduced here because they all include evidence that one of the LSAs has noticed something about the child's response.

Open discussion

In these incidents the LSAs raised issues as soon as they arose and in the hearing of the teacher.

Coins in a jar
The children were sitting on the mat and working on counting activities. One activity involved 2p coins being dropped in a glass jar. The children had to close their eyes and count in twos in their heads, using the sound of the coins dropping in the jar. When 12p was dropped in the jar, Neil said it was 22p and Claire said 10p. Most others seemed to get the correct answer.

The next example was 20p. Only three hands went up at the end, two of them offering the correct answer. The next example was 14p. Several incorrect answers were offered, for example 12, 16, 22, 31. The next example was 18p and this again led to several incorrect answers.

At this point the teacher and Mrs Taylor started to discuss the activity. They seemed surprised at the difficulty the children had with this compared to similar activities. They talked about the fact that the children did better with numbers up to 10 and concluded that they needed to concentrate on counting in 2s between 10 and 20 in future activities.

The end of the discussion between the two adults suggests that they were trying to work out on the spot what it might be about the activity that proved difficult for the children. Similar short discussions occurred on other occasions. These often amounted to a comparison of two activities. One example of this was counting alone rather than as a group. Another example was counting in fives starting from a higher number rather than zero or five. Explanations for difficulties were not always forthcoming. One week the teacher admitted to being 'mystified' when the children appeared to have difficulty with a counting activity which they had managed on other occasions. The discussion above suggests that an idea arose about possible activities for the future. Incidents where the adults talked about possible next steps occurred in other lessons. Sometimes the next step was immediate. For example, on one occasion the teacher was leading a practical session on addition with the intention of moving on to a related worksheet. The practical session proved harder going than expected and the adults agreed between them that they would abandon the plan to do the sheet that day. Instead the teacher introduced a number card activity on addition which was an intermediate step between the practical activities and the worksheet.

In all the examples above, the adult discussion was about the responses of the group in general to an activity. Occasionally the adults talked about how individual children were responding to an activity. An example is given below.

Spider
The children were on the mat and the teacher was leading an activity using a large hundred square and a plastic spider which she moved around the square. The children started by being asked the number 10 more than the one the spider was on. Later questions included 20 and 30, more and less.

At one point the spider was on 64. The teacher said that his dinner was on '20 more' and the children had to say which number this was. Douglas was asked but said he was not sure and didn't give a number. Other children then answered correctly.

The activity continued with different examples and Mrs Carrington helped Douglas, who was sitting near her. A little later she told the teacher that she thought Douglas was 'struggling' and asked if he could move nearer to the hundred square so he could touch it. The teacher initially agreed, but then had the idea of giving Douglas a smaller hundred square to work with. She handed the hundred square to Mrs Carrington, who worked with Douglas on the next examples using it. Neil, who was sitting nearby, also made some use of it.

The next example was 20 less than 55. Douglas continued to have problems. He seemed to be moving in ones rather than tens and said to Mrs Carrington, 'I'm looking at the next door neighbour numbers.' After a few more examples, Douglas was getting the right answers and was encouraged by Mrs Carrington to put his hand up and answer.

Looking back at this incident, I wonder whether Mrs Carrington started watching Douglas when he didn't give an answer to the teacher's earlier question. Because her intervention was made immediately, Douglas was given something to help him with subsequent examples – raising the matter afterwards would not have had this effect. However, provision of the hundred square did not enable Douglas to answer the questions straight away. What it did do was to give the adults more information about his difficulty, enabling him to be helped further. After further help and encouragement from Mrs Carrington, Douglas was able to answer the questions correctly. Provision of the hundred square was also of help to Neil. This suggests that what appears to be a difficulty confined to one child may be more widespread. This incident also suggests shared values between the teacher and Mrs Carrington in wanting to help the children understand the mathematics, rather than just giving the correct answer.

A potential problem with this example, however, is that it involves an individual child's difficulty being discussed very openly. Perhaps for this reason, individuals were sometimes discussed by the adults before or after the lesson when the children weren't there – something which will be considered in the next section.

Discussion outside lessons

Although it seemed quite usual in the classroom for short adult discussions to take place as issues arose, they also sometimes happened briefly before and after lessons. After-lesson discussions sometimes occurred when adults informed each other about children they had worked with individually or in small groups. Before-lesson discussions arose when the teacher said what was planned for the lesson, and speculation followed about possible outcomes and possible changes. An example of an after-session discussion is given below.

Smartie graphs
The lesson had just finished. The main activity had been to draw a graph of colours from a tube of Smarties. The children had gone to play, taking their Smarties with them. The adults were putting the graphs in the children's folders.

Mrs Taylor, who had worked on the same table as James, talked about how well he had done today. She said he needed less help than expected with the graph and she thought he really understood what he was doing.

This led to a discussion of James and how much he can do by himself. Mrs Carrington, who usually works with James, talked about some other incidents. She said that although she was there to work with him, she wanted to encourage his independence rather than sit with him every minute.

The after-lesson discussions did not have the immediate impact that on-the-spot discussions had, but they did have some advantages. One was that there was more time. Although these discussions were usually of only a few minutes duration and were often carried out while the adults were cutting things out or putting things away, they were still longer than the few exchanged sentences which were possible during lessons without losing teaching time. Confidentiality was another advantage, and mathematical problems of individuals rather than apparently 'whole group' problems were more commonly raised in this way.

The discussion about James and the Smartie graphs moved on from reporting back on his work to discussing a key issue, that of how LSAs assigned to individual children maintain the balance between helping them and encouraging their independence. There were other occasions when reports of incidents turned into discussions of issues. For example, towards the end of the spring term, Mrs Taylor had been asked by the teacher to carry out assessments of individuals against a list of items. At the end of the lesson Mrs Taylor told us that Douglas had appeared to have great difficulty with the items, for example failing to tell her the number after 88. The rest of us talked about things we had seen Douglas do on that day and other days. This led to speculation about why some of the children performed inconsistently. We also talked about whether it is fair to base assessment on performance on a particular day, especially if it contradicts observations made on other days.

Major issues were also sometimes discussed as a result of reflecting on how a particular task went, or talking about what would be done next. One such discussion was about how much time should be spent on consolidation and whether children should still be moved forward if they seemed to have difficulties with current work. Also discussed was the difficulty children had when activities were varied, for example from counting in twos to counting in fives or from adding to subtracting. The teacher and the LSAs talked about whether it was legitimate to keep the activity the same in the hopes that children might keep getting correct answers. They contrasted this with the hope that children should be able to respond to variations in the task rather than just repeating the same thing. None of these discussions were apparently planned; they arose naturally from a situation where the adults talked openly to each other about the children's responses to the work.

Action without consultation

In the examples above, the LSAs suggested changes to the teacher and hence I was aware of their suggestions. It is obviously harder to know whether they made any changes to tasks without saying anything, though on the occasions when I worked close to another adult, I sensed that it was considered acceptable to make minor changes according to how the activity was going. Often these were mentioned in casual discussion afterwards. I did note one example where I was aware that the LSA decided to adapt an activity for a particular child.

> *Dice addition*
> The children were working at the tables. Each child had three dice, a number line to 20 and their maths book. The task was to throw the die, write the sum and find the answer, using the number line if needed. There was an adult on each table.
>
> Mrs Carrington, who was working on the table next to mine, asked me if there was a spare die on our table. She said that she thought Kate could do the activity with four dice.

Reflecting on this incident, I recalled that there were other occasions when LSAs suggested that children got pieces of equipment to help them, without asking the teacher. I also noticed that when children were working on 'early work' activities before the main lesson started, adults would ask extension questions of some children who appeared to do the tasks easily. It seemed to be accepted practice for LSAs to provide support or extension for tasks, albeit in small ways, without necessarily asking or telling the teacher.

Other issues

Most of the incidents described above refer to whether or not children seemed able to do the tasks provided. Sometimes the issue of time needed for a task arose. There was some flexibility here, with LSAs occasionally judging that a child needed more time to complete a task as the others returned to the mat, and this was usually agreed with the teacher.

It will be clear from the incidents above that there was a good working relationship between the adults in the classroom. There was also a certain amount of shared humour. One apparent consequence of this was that it was possible to diffuse potentially embarrassing situations. If a mistake was made or an answer forgotten by the adults, one of the others was usually able to step in under the shared joke that we were having a bad day or had forgotten where we were up to.

Discussion

Impact on mathematics

The incidents above suggest that the way this classroom team worked together had some impact on the mathematics. Sometimes the impact was fairly direct and obvious, for example in the 'spider' example. In this example, adult intervention enabled Douglas's difficulties to be considered more closely and then enabled Douglas, and possibly Neil, to succeed with a task which he had originally not seemed able to do. Similarly, in the case of Kate and the dice game, adult intervention enabled her to work on a slightly harder task when the original one seemed easy for her.

Sometimes the effect of intervention was more subtle. For example, in the 'coins in the jar' and similar incidents, the combined views of the adults were used to inform decisions about what might be done immediately, or in subsequent lessons, or how activities might be altered. The combined views of the adults were also sometimes used to consider the strengths and difficulties of individuals, usually in discussions outside the lesson. The success of this team in considering and acting on pupil difficulties is notable, as these areas are highlighted in recent reports as things teachers are finding difficult. For example, one evaluation of the implementation of the Numeracy Strategy suggests some teachers have difficulty in diagnosing and responding to individual differences in pupil understanding (Earl, Levin, Leithwood, Fullan and Watson, 2001). A similar point is made in another evaluation of the Numeracy Strategy (OfSTED, 2001), which talks about the need to move from noticing pupils' responses to acting upon them, perhaps in subsequent lessons. It is further suggested that diagnosing and subsequently addressing pupils' misunderstandings is the key to higher standards. It seems that the team of adults in the case study is able to focus on an aspect of teaching that many teachers are finding difficult to address.

Finally, on an even more subtle level, the climate of open discussion and sharing of views often led the team of adults to reflect on and consider important and complex questions. Issues such as how much help LSAs should give children they are assigned to and how much children with learning difficulties should be encouraged to move forward, seemed to flow naturally from discussions about incidents during lessons.

Contrasting examples

In other classrooms I have been present in as a researcher, where expectations of adult intervention were different, similar incidents have occurred with different consequences. For example, there have been incidents where a child has gone through much of a lesson unable to do a series of tasks, where there was an adult who saw the difficulty and could think of a way of adapting the task, but felt she was not 'allowed' to do so. Similarly, LSAs have held back from offering extensions or extra challenges to children who have completed work easily.

Sometimes I have noticed adults venturing their opinions after lessons early in the year, only to stop doing so when it seemed their views were not valued or acted on. Similarly, in such classrooms there has been little conversation between teacher and LSAs about the children's response to the mathematics, though sometimes LSAs working in the same class held such discussions between themselves without involving the teacher.

Factors influencing approaches

The case study given here has many positive features. Nevertheless, it is given as an example not as an 'only' or even 'best' approach, as any way of working has potential disadvantages. How a team decides to work together will depend on many factors and will vary between classes and schools. Although it is not possible to show for certain what factors enabled this team to work in the way described, it is worth speculating a little on this. Certainly the LSAs had the mathematical knowledge and understanding to make useful contributions. Perhaps more importantly, the teacher was aware of this knowledge and understanding and valued it. This may be because she took time to talk to the LSAs and got to know their strengths. It is also worth noting that the LSAs were involved in numeracy training within the school, meaning that all the teachers had some awareness of the knowledge of the LSAs, and also meaning that LSAs and teachers were likely to share some understanding of issues and approaches. Personal factors are also clearly important. Matters were helped by the teacher's openness to ideas as well as by the fact that the adults appeared to get on well socially and to value each other's views and experiences.

Conclusions

The case study outlined above supports the view that children's learning is enhanced if use is made of the observations of LSAs. In this case study classroom, an atmosphere had been established where LSAs felt free to comment on or act upon their observations. As a result, the adults worked effectively as a team, doing their best to diagnose and act on children's difficulties. Their teamwork was also evident in their discussion of complex issues related to teaching, supporting and assessing pupils with learning difficulties. The views of the LSAs were not just 'valued' by the teacher in an abstract sense – they were welcomed and made use of.

The team described here had established a way of working together which meant that LSAs sometimes contributed when the teacher was talking to the class, and it was not seen as disrespectful or undermining to the teacher for them to do so. In contrasting cases, opportunities were missed when LSAs held back, perhaps out of respect for the teacher's authority. My findings suggest that what is needed is for teachers also to respect the views of LSAs. If their views are sought and valued, children's learning is likely to be enhanced.

References

APLIN, R. (1998) *Assisting Numeracy: A handbook for classroom assistants.* London: Beam.

BALSHAW, M. (1999) *Help in the Classroom (Second Edition).* London: David Fulton Publishers.

DfEE (1999) *The National Numeracy Strategy: Framework for Teaching Mathematics from Reception to Year 6.* Sudbury: DfEE Publications.

EARL, L., LEVIN, B., LEITHWOOD, K., FULLAN, M., WATSON, N. with TORRANCE, N., JANTZI, D. and MASCALL, B. (2001) *Watching and Learning 2, OISE/UT Evaluation of the Implementation of the National Literacy and Numeracy Strategies.* Toronto: Ontario Institute for Studies in Education, University of Toronto.

FARRELL, P., BALSHAW, M. and POLAT, F. (1999) *The Management, Role and Training of Learning Support Assistants.* Nottingham: DfEE Publications.

FOX, G. (1998) *A Handbook for Learning Support Assistants: Teachers and assistants working together.* London: David Fulton Publishers.

HOUSSART, J. (2001) Counting difficulties at Key Stage 2. *Support for Learning,* 16(1), 11–16.

Ofsted (2001) *The National Numeracy Strategy: The second year: an evaluation by HMI.* London: Ofsted.

ROBBINS, B. (2000) *Inclusive Mathematics 5–11.* London: Continuum.

TENNANT, G. (2001) The rhetoric and reality of learning support in the classroom: towards a synthesis. *Support for Learning,* 16(4), 184–8.

THOMAS, G. (1992) *Effective Classroom Teamwork, Support or Intrusion?* London: Routledge.

CHAPTER 13

Responsive questioning in a mixed-ability group

MUNDHER ADHAMI

A planned whole-class activity is normally structured around some given questions and guidance that steer pupils towards generalisations, connections and higher order thinking in the context or topic. These can be seen as *strategic* questions, formulated through analysis of task on the one hand, and judgements on the range of attainments or more general reasoning ability in a class on the other.

But the main job of teaching involves a different type of question that can be termed *tactical*, which, while guided by a strategic question at any given time, is couched in the particular pupils' responses, and which involves negotiation of meaning, handling of misconceptions and attention to minute and idiosyncratic steps of reasoning. Both type of questions can be seen as *responsive*, but while one is general and pre-defined, the other is specific, dynamic and creative.

Background

Many teachers use whole-class activities that allow all pupils to contribute and be challenged in their own terms, but also in collaboration with others. A useful resource in this field is the set of *Thinking Maths* (TM) lessons (Adhami, Johnson and Shayer, 1998a; 1998b; 1998c). This programme of lessons for use in Key Stage 3 is intended to challenge pupils across the ability range, with the focus on reasoning rather than on knowledge. The aim is to develop pupils' thinking ability through the structured exploration of major mathematical concepts in the main topic areas.

Any planned lesson is normally structured around a number of ideas or concepts, deemed significant in a topic area. In a TM lesson, the network of closely related concepts is explored through the sharing of different pupils' ideas in natural language and in a variety of informal or formal ways. But in addition the teacher must also channel the ideas in a trajectory of progression in logical reasoning towards higher order thinking. The emphasis on reasoning and natural language rather than on formal knowledge allows seemingly low attaining pupils to handle higher order ideas through informal expressions.

The activity is structured through suggested written questions in notesheets on which pupils jot down their ideas as reminders for sharing with the rest of the class. But the approach relies on other questioning by the teacher and other adults during *whole-class preparation, independent pair or group work* and *whole-class sharing*. A TM lesson will typically have two full cycles of this three-phase model, referred to in the methodology as episodes. Each phase has a different thinking agenda, and the teacher must take into account both the need for covering the intended agenda in the time allowed and engaging pupils' thoughts and motivation while they explore the concepts in their own ways. The role of such questions and the structure and planning is an essential aspect of the *Thinking Maths* approach.

The material provided for the teachers on each TM lesson comprises: a suggested lesson plan for a mainstream mixed-ability class; background notes on the mathematics and typical pupils' thinking processes in the task and topic found in trials; and detailed guidance for optimal flow of the lesson, providing challenges at an appropriate level for each individual or group of pupils. There will be different outcomes/achievements for different pupils in each lesson activity. There are 'prizes for all' (to quote from Alice). Hence we talk about the *agenda* of a lesson rather than its *objective*.

Strategic questioning

A sequence of strategic questions acts as the spine of the lesson as a whole. As discussed earlier, these are planned to match the range of demands in the task with the range of reasoning in the age group. The teacher may well adjust these to suit their knowledge of the class, so ends up with their own set of strategic questions. But there is still the need, in the classroom, to provide orally other, tactical questions in response to what the particular pupils offer at any one moment in the lesson. We will first discuss the strategic, or steering question, and move to tactical questions later.

The sequencing of strategic questions in CAME (Cognitive Acceleration in Mathematics Education)[1] lessons can be likened to those proposed by Watson and Mason (1998), a sequence of questions provoking successive steps of thinking. Watson and Mason assume that questioning can lead to higher order thinking and access to mathematical structure. One possible distinction between their work and the approach espoused here is in the starting point of the classroom enquiry. A TM lesson normally starts from experiential or familiar situations addressed in natural language, *concrete preparation*, which is then mathematised in a constructive trajectory, rather than starting within mathematical discourse.

Strategic questions on correlation across the ability range

The National Curriculum (DfEE/QCA, 1999) level descriptions by attainment targets include the statement, 'Pupils draw conclusions from scatter diagrams and have a basic understanding of correlation' at level 6, and the statement, 'They draw a line of best fit on a scatter diagram, by inspection' at level 7. In 1998 Key Stage 3 results, 36% of pupils achieved an average level 6 and above. It is understandable therefore that most work schemes for so-called 'middle' and 'lower' ability pupils in Key Stage 3 would not include correlation. However, all pupils benefit from handling concepts in flexible ways and, indeed, are entitled to meet concepts in order to develop their general mathematical thinking ability. Lesson observations in the main study phase of the research programme indicated that almost all pupils were able to contribute in lessons on correlation in Year 8.

---

1 The Cognitive Acceleration in Mathematics Education (CAME) programme of research and development in the secondary school spans the period 1993–1999 (CAME I, funded by The Leverhulme Trust, 1993–1995; CAME II, funded by The Esmée Fairbairn Charitable Trust and the ESRC, 1995–1997; and CAME Enhancement, funded by the King's College Research Strategy Fund, 1997–1999). Current work of the research team includes secondary professional development programmes for teachers and tutors and the extension of the research activity into the upper years of the primary school (as one project in the Leverhulme Numeracy Research Programme based at King's College London).

The first in the sequence of three lessons on correlation involves the use of an incomplete set of data in familiar contexts. On trialling it was found to have an agenda that was particularly appropriate for lower and middle achieving pupils (as well as higher achieving pupils).

The first episode deals with the weekly profit and losses made by a newly opened local shop (see Figure 1).

The main objective is for pupils to struggle with the presence of a pattern that is not exact but still possible to use intuitively. They then describe it mathematically, by constructing an upper and lower line, and a 'most likely' or 'most appropriate/useful' pattern line. The first three questions are strategic. The objective is for the pupils to recognise that, although they cannot predict the value exactly, they can still make a judgement using an intuitive pattern of the data, and deal with a range of possibilities with different degrees of likeliness. This probabilistic thinking seems necessary for understanding the concept of correlation, including the meaning of the line of best fit as an estimated mathematical construction.

The *key* strategic question in the notesheet is no. 3. Rather than only posing this, however, the TM approach structures the investigation, both in time and in focus or direction of mental activity, in order to pose successive challenges across the ability range in a class. The responses observed during the lesson trials, and by teachers since, have confirmed its value in steering thought and discussion towards predicting intuitively the most likely upper and lower limits of an appropriate guess for this missing value.

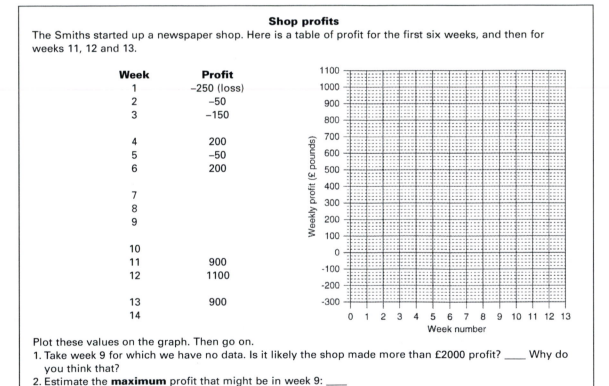

Shop profits

The Smiths started up a newspaper shop. Here is a table of profit for the first six weeks, and then for weeks 11, 12 and 13.

Week	Profit
1	−250 (loss)
2	−50
3	−150
4	200
5	−50
6	200
7	
8	
9	
10	
11	900
12	1100
13	900
14	

Plot these values on the graph. Then go on.

1. Take week 9 for which we have no data. Is it likely the shop made more than £2000 profit? ____ Why do you think that?
2. Estimate the **maximum** profit that might be in week 9: ____
   And the **minimum** it might be? ____
3. What do you think the **most likely** profit at the end of week 9? ____
   How did you arrive at this?
4. At what week would you have felt the shop is not going to lose money any more?
5. How would you describe the pattern of the profit? What additions can you make to the graph picture to show that pattern?
6. What do you think the likely pattern from week 14 onwards might be?

Figure 1. Correlation notesheet

In order to approach the notion of likelihood, however, there needs to be other *subsidiary* (strategic) questions, here questions 1 and 2, and also further elaborating questions, here from no. 4 onwards, to place any insights gained within a fuller understanding of links between the individual bits of data, the total mathematical model, and the real context itself. These must also be regarded as strategic questions, since they are: a) predetermined as part of the agenda to the lessons; and b) necessary for the move to exploring the key question.

Similar distinction between key and subsidiary strategic questions can be seen in the second episode (see Figure 2). This episode explores the new concepts further in a context which extends the activity to allow for a deeper mathematical understanding of data, and the rationale for the line of best fit. Here the key question (number 1) is again general and open.

That is followed by a number of elaborating questions which go some way to quantifying the relationship in terms of ranges. The placement of strategic questions on the notesheet provides the teacher and the pupils with the framework of the lesson.

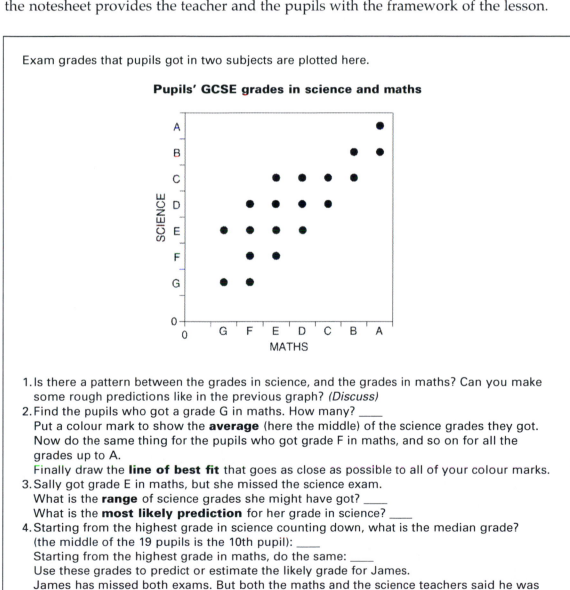

Exam grades that pupils got in two subjects are plotted here.

Pupils' GCSE grades in science and maths

1. Is there a pattern between the grades in science, and the grades in maths? Can you make some rough predictions like in the previous graph? *(Discuss)*
2. Find the pupils who got a grade G in maths. How many? ____
   Put a colour mark to show the **average** (here the middle) of the science grades they got. Now do the same thing for the pupils who got grade F in maths, and so on for all the grades up to A.
   Finally draw the **line of best fit** that goes as close as possible to all of your colour marks.
3. Sally got grade E in maths, but she missed the science exam.
   What is the **range** of science grades she might have got? ____
   What is the **most likely prediction** for her grade in science? ____
4. Starting from the highest grade in science counting down, what is the median grade? (the middle of the 19 pupils is the 10th pupil): ____
   Starting from the highest grade in maths, do the same: ____
   Use these grades to predict or estimate the likely grade for James.
   James has missed both exams. But both the maths and the science teachers said he was 'about average' in the class. What do you think his grade could be? ____
5. What are the advantages and disadvantages of the mathematics of correlation? ____

Figure 2. Correlation: maths and science notesheets

Tactical responsive questioning

The strategic questions, however detailed, are not sufficient on their own. Pupils' responses to any strategic question may throw open some misconceptions and naive ideas, the treatment of which may be essential to further flow of the lesson in the given classroom. That would require another type of questions that can be termed *tactical responsive questions*, since they are not predetermined but rather contingent on particular pupils' responses. It is these that can be regarded the more difficult to formulate since consideration of time, loss of focus, potential for successive diversions from lesson agenda, can all impinge on the actual steering of the exchange of ideas in the direction of the strategic question.

Some tactical questions can often be anticipated through practice, linked to the common misconceptions and misunderstanding in a topic in any given age group and a given culture. But responsiveness requires the teacher to phrase consecutive oral questions using, largely, the actual phrases offered by the youngsters for the preceding ones, with or without appropriate paraphrasing, thereby letting them retain their sense of ownership of the developing ideas as well as maintaining their cognitive engagement with the task. The starting point for any genuine cognitive activity has to be children's own concrete and familiar experiences, which can be idiosyncratic, hence the likely great diversity of the flow of questioning in different classes around the same strategic question.

Tactical responsive questions are based on generic questioning techniques (for example, the necessary wait time for pupil's answer, and for answer elaboration through further wait time, repeat and further question such as 'What do you mean?', 'When, where, why, how, does that happen?' etc.), but are also distinct in that their forms require specific substance to have value beyond pupils' mere participation.

Example on tactical questions around one strategic question

The group of pupils

The following scene is a reconstruction of a discussion with a group of Year 8 and Year 9 pupils attending a Saturday session in Hillingdon. This class of about 65 pupils from different schools included pupils working at below average NC levels. From my experience, such low-to-middle attaining pupils who are willing to be challenged through working with more able peers tend to be relatively confident and even argumentative, but they may also rely on the more able in their group to formulate ideas for contribution to whole-class discussion.

Having started the class on formulating ideas in response to the questions about the shop profits, and being satisfied that they needed no help in plotting the points, I chose to work with the smallest and noisiest of the groups. This was a group of five boys, four of whom were working in pairs, and the fifth working noisily on his own sheet, interacting jokingly with the rest who seemed to be reacting with a mixture of tolerance and exasperation. I asked them to tell me the first ideas that come to their minds, and even any possible answers that they may feel to be wrong, indicating that I was specifically interested in how pupils moved from these first ideas to more refined ideas. The result was a kind of guided brainstorming session, which I believe is occasionally an effective teaching strategy. The lone boy's half-serious contributions were also useful to explore.

Limits to the graph

Three answers to question 1 were given quickly by this group, who seemed eager to engage in the game of producing different low level answers:

a. *No, because we don't have 2,000 on the graph.*
b. *No, because it goes down in odd numbers, or because it is down on 7, then up on 8, so will be down in 9.*
c. *No, because it is too far, too high, doesn't fit.*

The account below is not an actual transcription, but it does represent a reasonable reconstruction of the interaction based on notes written shortly after the event. In addition, it has been confirmed by teachers who have also taught the lesson as realistic and typical of responses of pupils struggling with the concepts involved.

Response (a) above is typical of lower attaining pupils constrained by the concrete limitations of the available graph, and not assimilating yet that any graph is a restricted view of an infinite abstract grid. Teachers often cite the limit of the graph on the page as a response they expect from lower attaining pupils. This can be easily and quickly brushed aside or corrected by the teacher or a more able pupil saying, for example, 'You can imagine the graph bigger if you need it.' On the other hand the teacher may wish to engage with this misconception fully.

T. Let's take the first idea about how far the graph goes.
P. *I was only kidding, Sir.*
T. But it is an interesting idea. It is true we cannot plot the £2,000 on this graph if that happens, so what can we do about it?
P. *We can draw more lines above.*
   We need more paper to reach 2,000.
T. You mean we can extend the graph upward as far as that by adding more paper? Can we reach 3,000 or 10,000?
P. *Yes, you can reach a million if you want.*
   You will need a lot of paper!
T. Interesting. Are you saying you can extend the graph only if we have paper? Suppose we use just imagination. How far can we imagine the graph extended?
P. *As far as you want.*
   You can go for ever.
   You won't have enough paper in the whole world.
T. If we are imagining, we don't need the paper, do we? So you think we can go for ever. What does that mean, 'go for ever'?
P. *Into space.*
   To the moon and stars. Past the sun. Galaxies. Alpha Centauri.
   Infinity.
T. So the graph in our mind is infinite. What does infinity mean? Is it a real number?
P. *It is trillion billion billion zillion . . .*
   Cannot reach it.
   A number that you cannot write. Imaginary. Complex. Irrational.
T. Wah. We are going all over the place. The main thing is that however large a number you reach you can always twice it, or ten times it, or . . .

This scene took between two and three minutes, but covered important ideas. Pupils often have ideas which allow fruitful diversions from the main agenda. Engaging with such ideas, or not, is an *optimisation decision* for teachers and other supporting adults, that is, balancing the greatest active mental involvement by the pupils, at the highest level of thinking possible with them, together with the manageability of the overall flow and agenda of the lesson. In this scene, with a little more time, I could have expanded the interaction by following on from the need for more paper with a question such as: 'How much paper do we need for the graph to reach 2,000? or 10,000?', thereby addressing ratio visually or through mental imagery, and using multiplicative relations to construct the size of larger and larger numbers using the idea of unitising 'easy large numbers', leading again to infinity. This did not occur to me at the time, however, and taking this on board may well have been too great a diversion from the main agenda, making it difficult to return to the main strategic questions.

Pupils here are exploring the meaning of infinitely large numbers and expressing it in informal or haphazard formal language about types of numbers. I was not sure how to help them, therefore I moved away from that line of thinking. I think the problem here is that working inductively or constructively from natural language descriptions of experiential activity seems easier than working with inappropriate associations with formal ideas, such as the complex or irrational numbers to which pupils often resort when guessing at random, possibly to impress! Did we need to explore each of these high level formal concepts? It is probably not important that they reach a conclusion on the issue of infinity, or use the right technical terms; just raising their curiosity was sufficient. Further exploration would be a diversion in the present lesson, and it can be argued that following such diversion, some pupils will remain mentally occupied with the new concepts and therefore distracted from the main agenda of the lesson. Notions of infinity are not explicitly assessed or even addressed in the mathematics curriculum. On the other hand, such pupils would be thinking mathematically at a level appropriate for them, motivated and curious, and these concepts are of importance for the nature of the subject and for many higher order concepts.

Joining dots versus overall pattern

I switched to the mention of odd numbers. Two pairs have joined the dots, and one pair with faint lines of continuing the pattern (see Figure 3).

T. Now the other idea, about the odd number of weeks. What do you mean?
P. *It goes up and down. Zigzag. Buying stock every other week, odd weeks. More profit in even weeks.*
T. So could it be £2,000 on week 8?
P. *Could be. Yes. Not likely. Too steep. Week 8 should be less than 900.*
T. How do you know it's not likely? And less than 900? If it is a zigzag then it can go up and you do not know how far, do you?
P. *There is a pattern. The zigzag has a pattern. It is going up but not too sharp.*
T. So the reason for saying 'No' is not really the zigzag, but the pattern of zigzag?
P. *Yeeeh (doubtful). Yes. Both.*

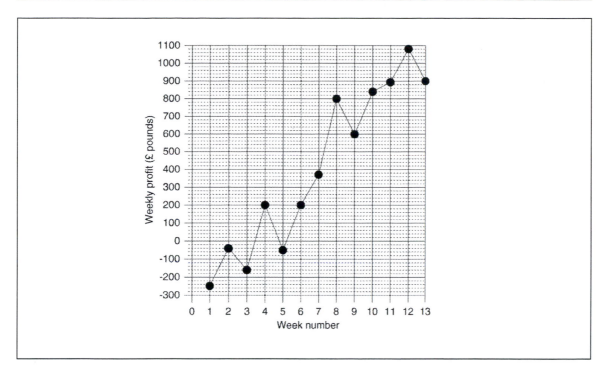

Figure 3. Pupils' work, with invention of possible values for weeks 7–10

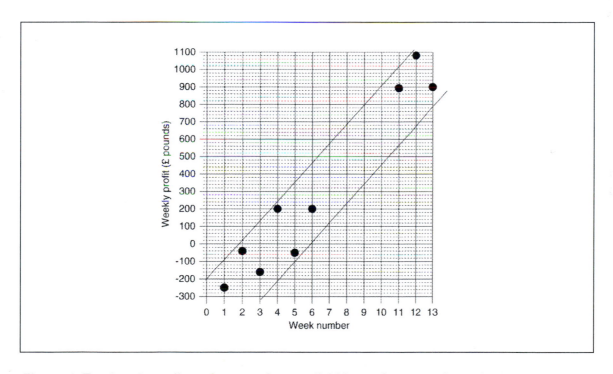

Figure 4. Teachers' two lines, interpreting pupils' ideas of a general trend

Pupils' naive strategies or learned responses of joining the dots in a graph were engaged here. It showed that the pupils have intuitively recognised the overall pattern, as well as the zigzag, and can interpret the data when related to familiar situations. One might ask what the responses would have been if the question had been about week 8 or week 10?

Imposing a structure

What followed was very brief (see Figure 4).

> T. Do we really need to join the dots for this kind of thinking?
> P. *(Hesitation.) You always join the dots to make a graph. Yes you do. Not really.*
> T. How can you show the overall pattern so that you can guess how far or how low it can be?
> P. *(Making diagonal movements on the graph, one with open forefinger and thumb). A kind of like this. Wiggly strip.*
> T. A strip. So there are two lines?
> P. *Yes, parallel lines. No, wiggly.*

I stopped at that point. The parallel and wiggly lines were a diversion I was not sure about.

Remainder of the lesson

In the whole-class plenary I used some of the ideas generated in discussion, and the idea of the strip was emphasised in collecting the answers to the next question, on the maximum and minimum values they thought the profit in week 9 could be.

The values for the maximum expected profit for week 9 ranged between £500 and £900, and the minimum expected between £300 and £600. I did not follow up on the reasoning behind these estimates, but rather focused on the middle value in each range and then the most likely value.

The cognitive demand here is to coordinate two patterns, one more concrete, given by the seesaw or zigzag, the other more abstract, given by a vague general linear rise in profits. To construct this second pattern requires weakening of the concrete pattern, and acceptance of values as approximate or as ranges. This is visually achieved by showing the suggested maxima and minima of expected profits by different groups of pupils, but then the middle values also need constructing, for example, by exploring the principle of suggesting a representative value that offers the least error.

How are the 'tactical' questions formed?

The examples above show that responsive questioning involves the teacher in managing the tension between the proposed agenda for a lesson and the range of ideas actually generated by the pupils in a particular class. Not an easy task, especially since the coordination at the 'ideas plane' has also to take into account the coordination of the 'social plane', that is, keeping pupils on task, and maintaining pace.

Responsive questioning can be seen as a to-and-fro flow of questions and answers. The process starts with a strategic question, that is, one dictated by the pre-defined agenda of the lesson, and which is suitable for different classes addressing the same agenda. All answers are acknowledged as valid or useful contributions. This is then followed with a related but more focused question, often through a shift of emphasis or paraphrasing of the pupils' contributions. The next question can be termed a tactical question since it represents an *ad hoc* response to the emerging conditions in the particular class, but this is still guided by the same agenda (see Figure 5).

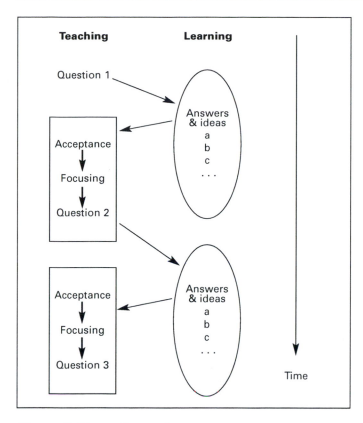

Figure 5. Flow of questions

The description of the interactions given in Figure 5 excludes the mental processes within the pupils and within the teacher and as such is very limited in its explanatory power. On each side there are internal mental processes. Pupils' responses to a question are dependent on the processing of the ideas and their subsequent interactions/contributions to the classroom discourse. The teacher's focusing is dependent on background knowledge, both of these aspects of pupils' thinking as well as on a flexible knowledge of the agenda of the lesson.

Teachers' *ad hoc* responsiveness and actions are based on background beliefs, explicitly and implicitly. We need to focus attention on the fact that each teacher and supporting adult has a more or less coherent view of cognition, of how people learn individually and in social settings (i.e. a 'learning theory') and also a more or less coherent set of values and beliefs of what is the right thing to do in any teaching/learning situation. When applied to a particular lesson, these general aspects are translated into a view of the agenda of the lesson, and the appropriate pedagogy for it.

The cognitive and the social in learning and development

The CAME approach follows in the steps of progressive mathematics educators of the past decades. In cognitive terms it attempts to contribute to the emphasis on the conceptual aspects of mathematics, and often goes beyond that to the exploration of more general reasoning aspects that are valid across conceptual clusters. It also attempts to integrate this emphasis with a mode of classroom work that emphasises inclusion, collaboration and autonomy of learners as groups and individuals, a contribution in social terms. The guidance materials, and studies such as this one, attempt to exemplify and make explicit how the two aspects of the approach interrelate in each component, such as in questioning.

One of the hypotheses in CAME is that the approach can only be developed further by teachers, and by educationists in general, through the conscious merging of theory and practice. Theory can be seen either as sets of generalisations from accumulated practice or as explanatory models originating from basic sciences applied in new contexts. Both of these interpretations are possible as descriptions for CAME. In shorthand one can point to the Piagetian and neo-Piagetian perspectives on the one hand, and to the Vygotskyan and social-constructivist perspectives on the other, as the two main sources of theory we use to distinguish, then to consciously attend to, how the two aspects of any classroom activity, the cognitive and the social, are integrated at any moment in time.

The cognitive aspect, or dimension, of an activity addresses the reasoning levels a) implicit in the mathematics, and b) characteristic of each pupil – which, in ordinary mathematics lessons, need to be well matched if there is to be a reasonable chance of the pupil mastering a skill or concept. A TM lesson is designed so that, for each pupil, the challenge is aimed ahead, but not too far, of their present cognitive level. The social constructivist aspect raises the question – given the cognitive aim of the lesson, what form of social interaction will best serve to achieve it?

Our answer to this question comes from Vygotsky's model of the *zone of proximal development*. Our belief is that cognitive development occurs through *mediation*: the learner, possessing a partial strategy, sees or hears in someone in her current social world the complete strategy applied to just that situation she is working on. She instantly assimilates this into her mental, including deeper processing, structures. This implies that the best mediators may be a child's fellows, because they are closer to him both in thinking and also in personal style. The teacher may desperately wish to model the solution for the child, but is usually too far beyond where the child presently is to be able to interact unless she relies on the child's own ideas and, simultaneously, with those of his/her peers. This is the rationale for the notion of responsive tactical questioning.

Implications for teaching

Hopefully the notions of a sequence of strategic or steering questions on the one hand and responsive or tactical questioning on the other informs the analysis of current good teaching practice. It seems possible to regard responsive questioning as the main and essential quality of good teachers. But there seems no easy route to develop such skills. Three main requirements for responsive questioning can be identified:

1. Flexible knowledge of the activity and topics involved, including common misconceptions, and the different connection that can be made from lower order to higher order concepts. Books on misconceptions (e.g. Dickson, Brown and Gibson, 1984) and guidance on well-designed lessons are helpful, in addition to reflection on practice.
2. Genuine acceptance and engagement with pupils' ideas in their own language. Based on (1) above these ideas can then be sifted and focused while pupils retain ownership and move in their thinking.

3. A sense of the 'optimum', or the 'best possible', decisions in a given classroom situation. Every class and every lesson is different, and teaching involves continuous adjustments in response to the unfolding scene. The teacher must engage with various contributions, at the same time keeping an eye on the overall agenda, and keep the momentum, and be aware of the time. A good lesson is one where most pupils have met personally meaningful challenges and moved in their thinking.

Interleaving the strategic and tactical questions allows us to avoid both the 'telling' approach on the one hand, and the 'Anything goes' approach, which on their own may result in pupils not working to their full potential.

References

ADHAMI, M., JOHNSON, D. and SHAYER, M. (1998a) Cognitive development and classroom interaction: a theoretical foundation for teaching and learning. In J. D. Tinsley and D. C. Johnson (eds), *Information and Communication Technologies in School Mathematics*. London: Chapman Hall, 205–13.

ADHAMI, M., JOHNSON, D. and SHAYER, M. (1998b) Does CAME work? Summary report on phase 2 of the Cognitive Acceleration in Mathematics Education, CAME, project. In *Proceedings of the British Society for Research into Learning Mathematics Day Conference, Bristol, 15 November 1997*. London: BSRLM, 26–31.

ADHAMI, M., JOHNSON, D. and SHAYER, M. (1998c) *Thinking Maths: The Programme for Accelerated Learning in Mathematics*. Oxford: Heinemann Educational Books.

DfEE/QCA (1999) *Mathematics: The National Curriculum*. London: DfEE/QCA.

DICKSON, L., BROWN, M. and GIBSON, O. (1984) *Children Learning Mathematics – A Teacher's Guide to Recent Research*. London: Holt Education.

WATSON, A. and MASON, J. (1998) *Questions and Prompts for Mathematical Thinking*. Derby: ATM.

CHAPTER 14

Inclusion and entitlement: equality of opportunity and quality of curriculum provision

MIKE OLLERTON

> Alpha children wear grey. They work so much harder than we do, because they're so frightfully clever. I'm really awfully glad I'm a Beta, because I don't work so hard. And then we are so much better then the Gammas and Deltas. Gammas are stupid. They all wear green, and Delta children wear khaki. Oh no, I don't want to play with Delta children. And Epsilons are still worse. They're too stupid to be able . . .
>
> (Huxley, 1932, p. 33)

Brave New Labour

Some 18 months prior to the 1997 general election, when the Labour Party was seeking to recast itself as New Labour, Tony Blair and David Blunkett began to make public their opposition to mixed-ability teaching. Shortly after the election this rhetoric was formulated into policy, the White Paper *Excellence in Schools* (DfEE, 1997), advocating:

> . . . setting pupils according to ability . . . as one way of modernising the comprehensive principle.

By the time the National Curriculum (DfEE/QCA, 1999) was published, this policy had become a clear educational directive and, significantly, was described as one way of engaging with the fundamentally important issue of inclusion. On 27 May 2000 *The Guardian* reported on leaked Labour policy forum documents which continued this attack on mixed-ability teaching:

> We want to see schools which focus on what works and abandon any residual dogmatic attachment to mixed-ability teaching.

The language here is interesting; it implies that mixed-ability teaching does not work, is a 'residue' and a 'dogma'. This in itself is a contentious, dogmatic statement denying the possibility that mixed-ability teaching can be effective. Such arguments debase rational debate. Patrick Wintour quotes from a speech by Tony Blair in which he spoke of his opposition to mixed-ability teaching, describing comprehensive education as 'one-size-fits-all' and calling for 'rigorous setting':

> . . . whereby the most talented pupils are grouped in a separate class.
>
> (Wintour, 2000)

Ironically, with regard to mathematics teaching, one would need to search far and wide to find any school that does not use setting beyond Year 7; indeed there is evidence of an increased amount of setting in Years 6 and 5 (Sukhanandan with Lee, 1998, p. 48).

In this chapter I will argue that setting by ability is anathema to any notion of inclusion; it is iniquitous and runs counter to wider principles of equality of opportunity and children's entitlement of access to learning. I shall argue that setting by ability lays the seeds of some children's disillusionment with education, is in part responsible for, as well as a manifestation of, underachievement and has consequential effects upon motivation and behaviour.

> Pupils may become discouraged when they are placed in a lower set.
>
> (DfEE, 1998, p. 55)

Earlier research suggests that mixed-ability grouping is:

> . . . associated with good relationships between pupils and between teachers and pupils, and with cooperative attitudes on the part of pupils . . . a high level of motivation was engendered among pupils of below average ability.
>
> (DES, 1978, p. 67)

This may have been written a little while ago now, but that does not make it 'dogma'.

Setting by 'measured ability' in mathematics classrooms

The word 'ability' is used freely in discourse about children in schools as a measure of their academic standing. References to high ability, low ability and average ability children are frequently made as though there exists a common understanding of what these measures mean. Statistically, an average can only be taken from data that have been measured using an absolute scale, such as time, weight, distance and so on. To attempt to define an 'average' child with regard to mathematical 'ability', which involves a very complex collection of skills, is not feasible.

> There is no such thing as the average child, don't presume to cater for it.
>
> (Mark, 1995)

Since the onset of National Curriculum testing, a child's ability has often been defined according to the outcome of a Key Stage test. Paper-and-pencil testing is, however, a flawed attempt to measure children's mathematical potential. If it means anything, it takes a snapshot of current attainment rather than potential. I argue that this is an attempt to place them on an 'ability' scale for organisational convenience and in an attempt to simplify highly complex issues (Cooper and Dunne, 2000, p. 14). Even more worrying is how, on the basis of such information, children are placed in ability groups. Once in an ability group, children are offered a curriculum that is either different in content or pace by comparison with those placed in other ability groups; the obvious outcome is that children in different ability groups will learn different amounts of mathematics. Of course different outcomes are inevitable whatever form of organisation is used; this is the basis of differentiated learning. However, questions about setting and the provision of different learning opportunities must be considered.

Some are:

- Who decides what levels of curriculum provision should be offered to different children?
- When, in terms of children's age, should such decisions be made?
- Upon what basis are decisions made?
- How accurate are such decisions?

The accuracy of judgements made in setting children by 'ability'

To attempt to draw lines above which some children are deemed to have demonstrated a certain level of 'ability' and below which other children have less 'ability', and to use such information to create sets, could be a major reason for children's under-achievement. This is because it is not possible to obtain a standard interpretation of 'ability' based upon a measuring device, such as a test, or by using teachers' judgements that inevitably vary with different teachers and are based upon an element of crystal-ball gazing. Were tests to be applied on a different day they may render a different set of results. Indeed, it would be an interesting experiment for departments that create Year 7 sets, according to the Key Stage 2 test results, to give the same children the same Key Stage 2 tests the following September, examine the results and consider whether they would produce the same set lists. This would not be the case (Watson, 2001). Furthermore, the notion of determining accurate, meaningful measures of a whole generation of children, according to how they respond to particular types of questions, whether they are realistic ('real life' context based) or esoteric questions (without a 'real life' context) has been thrown into dispute by Cooper and Dunne (2000, p. 199). Their research shows that children from different social-class backgrounds 'perform less well on "realistic" items in comparison with "esoteric" items'. To separate children by defining 'ability' according to scores achieved in tests which, if on a different day, or if different types of questions were asked, different results may be achieved, must be a serious cause for concern. Categorising children in such ways is self-fulfilling and consequently creates deep problems:

> If the child is defined as a failure he will almost certainly fail, at any rate in the things which the definers value; and perhaps later he will hit out very hard against those who so defined him. So we know at least something to avoid. But we must contrive to avoid it not merely at the surface of our behaviour. If we do not genuinely respect and value the children, I am afraid they will come to know.
>
> (Donaldson, 1978, p. 114)

Teachers clearly have an enormous responsibility for determining whether or not they choose to create 'ability' groups, particularly if the judgements they make are based upon transitory, changing information about children's understanding and achievements. Furthermore, children's achievements are strongly connected to teachers' expectations.

A rationale for separating children into 'ability' sets?

Both Tory and Labour governments' preference for using tests and league tables to measure children and schools is having the effect of lowering the age at which grouping by ability commences. Yet irrespective of how children are grouped, there will always be different depths of understanding. Even the most tightly setted classes will contain pupils with a mix of abilities. Attempts to produce homogenous learning groups, possibly to make teaching easier, shift the focus away from how children learn and away from the fact that different levels of cognition exist in any group. Indeed, attempts to minimise this differential through setting, to aim for greater homogeneity as a way of raising achievement, were questioned by the government's own Numeracy Task Force:

> When considering the scope for setting pupils, it is important for schools to remember that setting does not necessarily help close the overall range in attainment across sets over time.
>
> (DfEE, 1998, p. 55)

It could be argued that the differentiated outcomes at the end of the educational process are the proof of accuracy of setting; but these are products of the setting process and curriculum differentiation as much as they are products of anything innate in the pupils. Teachers target their teaching and the advice they give to pupils at particular levels of achievement. Who decides, when, and on what grounds, that different children are to receive different levels of curriculum input? Such decisions impact upon children's opportunities throughout their formal education and into adulthood. Teachers could decide instead to try to confound low expectations (which may have been created not by innate ability but by outside features of their lives, past teaching and hence past performance) by teaching for higher attainment. It is of interest here that one outstanding difference between lower and higher achieving countries in international tests is that the higher achieving countries are teaching harder mathematics to younger pupils than the lower achieving ones (Leung, 1995): higher expectations on their own can make a difference.

Setting: is it for children, teachers or for organisational purposes?

Decisions about why setting is needed are highly questionable. The statement that it is 'easier' to teach groups of children who are of a similar ability suggests a teaching approach that is best fitted to a specific range of children, and that wide variations in learning outcomes cannot be accommodated within the same classroom. This is, perhaps, more to suit existing teaching styles than to cater for children's learning opportunities. As such setting is a teacher-centred form of organisation. However, I believe that the purpose of education is to serve each child's needs, and not to fit them into 'ability' groups for the organisational convenience of the school.

> . . . the child is a living thing, with thoughts and beliefs, hopes and choices, feelings and wishes: helping the child with these must be what education is about, for there is nothing else to educate.
>
> (Pring, 1976, p. 92)

My view of education is that when children are taught in mixed-ability groups the teacher does not need to predetermine what any individual might achieve; there is no need to construct different ceilings of future achievement. Teachers do, of course, have to form opinions about who is likely to struggle and who will respond to further challenges, but responding in-the-moment during a lesson, or planning for such eventualities within the timespan of the next few lessons, is different from making such decisions, effectively, years in advance. A typical example from my practice when working with mixed-ability groups was that all pupils, including those with statements of special educational need, were able to work with concepts such as Pythagoras' theorem and trigonometry – concepts which traditionally are only taught to higher set pupils (see Chapter 6).

To allow potential access to the whole statutory curriculum for all pupils, it is necessary to consider issues of differentiated learning. When children are taught in sets, decisions about future achievement have, by definition, previously been taken; learning outcomes prescribed and ceilings of achievement defined. In this way, setting is akin to differentiating by 'fixed' ability grouping, yet:

> . . . central to the improvement of practice must be the recognition that no child's potential is fixed.
>
> (Bourne and Moon, 1994, p. 36)

Pupils' confidence to learn, and planning for differentiation in mixed-ability groups?

When learning takes place in an environment and belief system which values effort and struggle as more important than 'given ability', a substantial body of research shows that students respond with higher achievement and motivation (Dweck, 2000). If pupils see the task as that of learning as much as they can rather than performing finite, clearly defined tasks, they work harder.

Enhancing achievement is related to developing pupils' confidence, and this is dependent upon individuals' self-perception. When children are placed in sets this provides clear messages about where they are in the 'pecking order'. It guides pupils' self-perception and confidence in their ability:

> . . . if they lack confidence in their ability, they will try to avoid challenges and show little persistence . . . pupils who view ability in mathematics as changeable and incremental tend to have, as their goal, increasing competence . . . one of the most important things a teacher can do is to foster a view of ability in mathematics as incremental rather than fixed.
>
> (Askew and Wiliam, 1995, p. 28)

Teaching in mixed-ability groups has important implications for the kind of planning the teacher must do in order to take account of incremental learning and differentiated outcomes. One approach is to construct a range of starting points, each of which is simple enough for every pupil but also rich enough to be developed so different children can experience different depths of learning.

Mathematical content needs to be differentiated to match the abilities of the pupils, but according to the principle quoted from the Cockcroft report, this is achieved at each stage by extensions rather than deletions.

(DES, 1985, p. 26)

How this is managed is dependent on the professional craft of the teacher. The quality of the interactions a teacher has with a class, and the relationships so formed, have significant impact upon children's cognitive development, as well as the choice of content and teaching approaches. In terms of equality of learning opportunities, all children are entitled to be supported and challenged. 'Being challenged', however, does not mean that this can only happen to good effect when children of supposedly similar ability are taught together in the same classroom. There are many ways of challenging children who have a wide range of potential achievements through lesson planning and ongoing informal assessment in mixed-ability classrooms (Ollerton and Watson, 2001).

As an example of this I offer an outline of how I teach surface area and volume (Figure 1). The initial task is one I have used with Year 7 children, yet the extension tasks would stretch pupils following an A-level mathematics course. Choosing a place from which everyone in a class can start and subsequently develop in different ways is one of the teacher's chief responsibilities. The suggested starting point requires a great deal of whole-class discussion and some hands-on, practical experience with interlocking cubes such as *Multilink*.

The underlying mode of operation is problem-solving; in this way important process skills such as classifying and proving are worked on simultaneously with the central concepts of volume and surface area. Pupils are set a problem, or a puzzle, which they can all initially access so none are daunted and all can be challenged. This is a basis for learning mathematics in any classroom. As Gattegno (1963) said:

All I must do is to present them [the pupils] with a situation so elementary that they all master it from the outset, and so fertile that they will all find a great deal to get out of it.

(p. 63)

The model of constructing an accessible starting point and a range of extensions tasks can be applied to the entire statutory curriculum, such as Pythagoras, graphs and functions or trigonometry. The approach of providing both consolidation and extension tasks means that the teacher makes ongoing, in-the-moment, professional judgements. I form ideas about pupils who are likely to need consolidation work and who will need more complex problems, but I make these decisions according to what pupils are currently doing, there and then in the classroom. Sometimes I will be surprised, and some pupils will perform differently from expectations; in a mixed-ability group I can accommodate any misconceptions about a child's ability and can be proved 'wrong', often with pleasure and surprise. Such lessons provide the atmosphere which, according to Dweck (2000), promotes most energetic learning.

A further issue is that I do not need to concern myself with shifting pupils from one class to another. In a mixed-ability class all children, whatever their assumed 'abilities', can be catered for. I do not need to construct a notional class pace; in reality, there will be as many different working paces as there are children. I do not need to spend wasteful energy deciding who is 'average', 'below' or 'above' average, nor do I need to worry about the 'rigour' (whatever this might mean) of any decisions taken to create ability sets.

Starting point
Each pair of pupils is given 24 cubes and posed the problem of how many different cuboids they can make. Underpinning this problem is the notion that certain combinations of the factors of 24 when multiplied together make 24. (There are six solutions: $1 \times 1 \times 24$, $1 \times 2 \times 12$, $1 \times 3 \times 8$, $1 \times 4 \times 6$, $2 \times 2 \times 6$, $2 \times 3 \times 4$).

Extension tasks
The following extension tasks can be posed as and when appropriate:

- Trying to prove that all the possible cuboids have been made.
- Sketching each cuboid on isometric paper (triangular-dot grid paper).
- Writing the dimensions of each cuboid.
- Calculating the surface areas of each cuboid.
- Trying to find a way of calculating the surface area of a cuboid if the dimensions are known and, therefore, constructing a formula.
- Determining the minimum and maximum surface areas.
- Exploring what makes a surface large or small.
- Determining how many different cuboids there are and their surface areas beginning with 2 cubes and working upwards to, say, 24. This leads to prime numbers being extracted, i.e. a prime number of cubes will only have one solution, i.e. $1 \times 1 \times n$ (where n is prime).
- Generalising the result for surface area for the set of cuboids $1 \times 1 \times m$ ($m = 1, 2, 3, 4, \ldots$).
- Finding a cuboid whose surface area (SA) is exactly 100.
- Working out all the possible solutions for volume, $V = 60$ (lots of factors and solutions here).

For older pupils, say Year 10 or 11, I could pose a problem which leads on from the notion of minimum surface area such as removing the condition of working with integer dimensions (or determining the minimum surface area if plasticine was used instead of solid cubes).

Further problems, some of which would challenge A-level students, could be:

- If the volume remained constant and shape was a cylinder, what dimensions might it have?
- What dimensions will provide a cylinder with the minimum surface area? What about a pyramid?
- Consider the set of cylinders where (radius and height) $r + h = 20$. Using integer values, in the first instance, what different volumes can be made? What values of r and h produce the minimum V? There are opportunities here for graphing results
- Take two pieces of A4 paper. Roll one into a cylinder 'lengthways' and the second into a 'shorter' cylinder the other way. Which of these will produce the largest volume?
- Bringing a selection of different sized cylinders, such as tins of beans etc., can lead to an interesting optimisation problem of 'best' dimensions to maximise V and minimise SA.
- A cube of side length 6 cm has a volume of 216 cm^3 and a surface area of 216 cm^2. Are there any other cuboids whose volume in cm^3 is equal to its surface area in cm^2? What about cylinders?
- How can the volume of an octahedron, a dodecahedron or an icosahedron be calculated?

Figure 1. Teaching surface area and volume

In setted groups, however, because different concepts are taught to different groups, the curriculum becomes structured in terms of what content is taught rather than the depth of what is taught. For example some concepts, such as trigonometry, are only taught to pupils who are to be entered for higher level GCSE. This means some pupils will be offered a restricted curriculum according to the set they are placed in. Yet Bruner stated that:

> With respect to making accessible the deep structure of any given discipline, I think the rule holds that any subject can be taught to any child at any age in some form that is both honest and powerful.
>
> (1972, p. 122)

High expectations for all children

Inclusion and entitlement are strongly linked to equality of opportunity, and this is supported by high teacher expectation. In all classes there will be a range of outcomes; where all can contribute, all can gain. A deep-seated belief, upon which setting is often rationalised, is that high attaining pupils are held back by low attaining pupils. However, what any pupil achieves is partly due to a teacher's expectations and supported by the quality of planning and classroom management skills. As these skills are developed, the teacher is capable of applying them to any classroom situation, whether pupils are setted or in mixed-ability groups, yet, as Askew and Wiliam noted:

> Research also shows that high-attainers gain from mixed-ability collaborative work as much as any other pupils . . . If ability in mathematics is not a fixed entity . . . then grouping by attainment may mean that particular expectations are set up from which pupils will have great difficulty breaking free.
>
> (1995, p. 41)

Building pupils' confidence while maintaining high expectations is central to the issue of effective classroom practice. Organisational structures within a department are a further significant component. Providing all pupils with opportunities to be included is an identifiable and significant expectation. During a recent discussion on the issue of setting and mixed-ability grouping, a teacher commented: 'Well, we might as well put them all in the top set.' The remark was meant to be negative, yet if we can offer every pupil opportunities to work on 'top' set mathematics, and have high expectations that all are capable of high achievement, then this comment is indeed a powerful one. However, complacency in the 'top' set is a related problem if pupils feel that all they need to show is good performance on examination questions (Dweck, 2000).

A problem for many children is that once they are placed in a particular set, then this is most likely where they will stay and future potential is largely predetermined. The solution to this problem offered by proponents of setting is that movement between sets is carried out – but there are two clear anomalies here. Firstly, 'a child's chance of remaining in its initial grouping for the rest of its school career is 88–89%' (Dixon, 1999, p. 1). Secondly, those children who do transfer 'up' a set will be disadvantaged as they will not have covered the same concepts as their new classmates.

Recognising pupils' present achievements, rather than seeking to predetermine their future achievements, underpins my rationale for not setting, categorising or separating pupils into ability groups. Keeping an open mind about each child's potential is consistent with a belief that everyone can achieve; my responsibility as a teacher is to provide supportive conditions to make this possible. Children's attainment, interests, work rates and achievements change and develop at different speeds.

Criterion for setting: date of birth, socio-economic circumstances, gender and race

Evidence from a sample of 192 primary schools in the north west of England indicates that setting by some measure of 'ability' is on the increase for mathematics lessons and is occurring at a younger age and, in some cases, in reception classes (McSherry and Ollerton, 2002). If educational futures are being predicted so early it is important to look at what the implications are for such early setting, what kind of criteria are being used and how criteria are applied to such life-affecting decisions.

A survey carried out in Shropshire schools in 1994 indicates that a higher proportion of May to August born children was placed in the lower sets than in the higher. This raised a question about whether date of birth was an unwittingly applied criterion when decisions about setting were made (Ollerton, 1998). Although this was a small-scale survey, the results are supported by Sharp and Hutchinson:

> Children who are younger in the year group are likely to do less well than their older classmates . . . If decisions are made on the basis of KS1 data (e.g. allocation to sets or streams) these age-related differences could have longer-lasting consequences for the children concerned.
>
> (1997, p. 9)

Sukhnandan and Lee take this issue much further, and their review of research in this area suggests that other factors come into play:

> . . . homogeneous forms of grouping reinforce segregation of pupils in terms of social class, gender, race and age (season of birth). Consequently, low ability classes often contain a disproportionately large number of pupils from working-class backgrounds, boys, ethnic minorities and summer-born children.
>
> (1988, p. 43)

Setting thus creates its own miniature forms of elitism in terms of class, gender, race and birth date.

Conclusion

All children, irrespective of race or social class, no matter what they have achieved in the past, have contributions to make in the present and the future. A significant characteristic of working with pupils in mixed-ability groups is the value the teacher gives to the inevitably wide range of contributions. Offering some pupils extension tasks does not preclude others from being provided with an equal opportunity to develop their mathematics commensurate with their present cognitive level. Similarly, providing some pupils with extra consolidation and practice tasks does not mean that others cannot be provided with extension work.

At the centre of learning processes are children who have entitlements, rights, hopes and aspirations. As such, education must be implicitly, explicitly and intrinsically free from centralised government intentions to categorise and divide children in ways which, if applied to race or gender would be immoral and, if applied to our own children, totally unacceptable.

Inclusion is an equality of opportunity issue; this, in turn, relates to quality of access for all children to the statutory curriculum. Teaching children who have wide ranges of conceptual understandings, work rates, motivations, potentials, behaviours and aspirations, in inclusive, mixed-ability classrooms is not just feasible, it is ethically desirable.

References

ASKEW, M. and WILIAM, D. (1995) *Recent Research in Mathematics Education 5–16*, (Commissioned by Ofsted). London: HMSO.

BOURNE, J. and MOON, B. (1994) A question of ability? In B. Moon and A. Shelton Mayes (eds)., *Teaching and Learning in the Secondary School*. London: Routledge.

BRUNER, J. S. (1972) *The Relevance of Education*. Trowbridge: Redwood Press.

COOPER, B. and DUNNE, M. (2000) *Assessing Children's Mathematical Knowledge: Social class, sex and problem-solving*. Buckingham: Open University Press.

DES (1978) *Mixed Ability Work in Comprehensive Schools*. London: HMSO.

DES (1985) *Mathematics from 5 to 16*. HMI Series Curriculum Matters 3. London: HMSO.

DfEE (1997) *Excellence in Schools*. London: HMSO.

DfEE (1998) *The Implementation of the National Numeracy Strategy*. London: HMSO.

DfEE/QCA (1999) *Mathematics: The National Curriculum*. London: DfEE/QCA.

DIXON, A. (1999) A canker by any other name. *FORUM for promoting comprehensive education*, 41(1), 1.

DONALDSON, M. (1978) *Children's Minds*. London: Flamingo/Fontana.

DWECK, C. (2000) *Self-theories: Their role in motivation, personality and development*. Philadelphia: Psychology Press.

GATTEGNO, C. (1963) *For the Teaching of Mathematics* (Volume 1). Reading: Educational Explorers.

HUXLEY, A. (1932) *Brave New World*. London: Granada.

LEUNG, F. K. S. (1995) The mathematics classroom in Beijing, Hong Kong and London. *Educational Studies in Mathematics*, 29, 297–325.

McSHERRY, K. and OLLERTON, M. (2002) Grouping patterns in primary schools. *Mathematics in Schools*, 31(1), 5–7.

MARK, J. (1995) Masterclass. *Times Educational Supplement*, 28/7/95.

OLLERTON, M. (1998) Ministerial muddling over mixed-ability. *Mathematics Teaching*, 165, 5–7, December.

OLLERTON, M. and WATSON, A. (2001) *Inclusive Mathematics 11–18*. London and New York: Continuum.

PRING, R. (1976) Knowledge and schooling. In D. Gillard (1992), Educational philosophy: does it exist in the 1990s? *FORUM for Promoting Comprehensive Education*, 34(4), 3–19.

SHARP, C. and HUTCHISON, D. (1997) *How Do Season of Birth and Length of Schooling Affect Children's Attainment at Key Stage 1? A question revisited*. Slough: NFER.

SUKHNANDAN, L. with LEE, B. (1998) *Streaming, Setting and Grouping by Ability: A review of the literature*. Slough: NFER.

WATSON, A. (2001) *Changes in Mathematical Performance of Year 7 Pupils Who Were 'Boosted' for KS2 SATs*. Paper presented at the Annual Conference of the British Education Research Asssociation, University of Leeds (Abstracts p. 164).

WINTOUR, P. (2000) Blair plans schools revolution. *The Guardian*, 9 September.

Index